Source Book for Teaching English Overseas

Source Book for Teaching English Overseas

A Practical Guide for Language Assistants

MICHAEL LEWIS and JIMMIE HILL

Heinemann Educational Books
London

Heinemann Educational Books Ltd.
22 Bedford Square, London WC1B 3HH

LONDON   EDINBURGH   MELBOURNE   AUCKLAND
HONG KONG   SINGAPORE   KUALA LUMPUR
NEW DELHI   IBADAN   NAIROBI   JOHANNESBURG
EXETER (NH)   KINGSTON   PORT OF SPAIN

ISBN 435 28992 6
First Published 1981

Set in 10 on 12 point Times by Typesetters (Birmingham) Ltd.,
and printed in Great Britain
by William Clowes Limited, Beccles and London

Contents

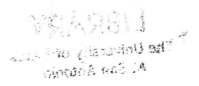

Acknowledgements

We would like to thank the following for permission to use material:

W. Foulsham and Co. Ltd for an extract from *Solve a Crime* by A. C. Gordon

Longman Ltd for an idea from *Teaching English as a Second Language* by J. A. Bright and P. G. McGregor

Folkuniversitets Forlag, Stockholm

Stadsmuseum, Stockholm

Paul Arthur, Visu-com Ltd, Toronto, and Dover Publications Inc., New York, for an illustration from *Handbook of Pictorial Symbols* by Rudolf Modley

Messrs Flick and Sons, Saxmundham

The British Tourist Authority

Peter Naylor

Introduction

You are going to spend next year working abroad as an assistant. What does that really mean? From your point of view, you probably see it mostly as a chance to improve your target language, and of course to enjoy the opportunity of spending a year living abroad. Many assistants feel that the dozen or so hours a week they have to spend teaching or giving conversation lessons, are almost incidental.

Most assistants are not (and probably don't want to be) language teachers. At the same time you probably have memories from your own school days of dreary 'conversations' started by an assistant asking 'What would you like to talk about then?' Unfortunately, most people's experience of conversation lessons is the same – rather artificial efforts to generate interest in a subject which perhaps nobody would be talking about if they weren't in that conversation class. This is hardly surprising. Very rarely even in our own language do we have conversations with 8, 12 or 16 people taking part, and not surprisingly even successful conversation lessons are usually dominated by two or three of the better pupils and, all too often, by the teacher.

Assistants in different countries and even in different schools can find themselves in very different situations. Some have small groups and some complete classes; some have only the older or more able pupils while others have youngsters of only 12 or 13 whose English is poor; some are in schools with good facilities and a helpful staff while others are not so lucky. Of course, you have to be prepared to adapt to the situation you find yourself in and it isn't very wise to try to swim directly against the tide. If the school has strong and clear ideas about what it wants you to do, it's obviously a good idea for you to do your best to follow those suggestions. In many cases, however, the school will be quite happy either to leave it to you or will only suggest 'conversation' lessons. In this book we try to give a range of activities

and materials that you will be able to use to make those conversation lessons something more than the rather dull and artificial topic-based classes you probably remember.

Our basic contention is that your year as an assistant offers both your pupils and you an invaluable experience. For both sides to get something out of it, what actually happens in the classroom must be taken more seriously by you than it has been by many in the past. In order to achieve this, we make three important assumptions. The first is that 'conversation lessons' should be both conversations and lessons. If you went to a swimming class, you would expect to do something more than just swim. You would expect guidance, advice, and instruction on how to get better. In our suggestions for your teaching, we have assumed that there is much more you can do than 'just let them talk'. Our second assumption is that the group of six highly motivated interesting eighteen-year-olds will be the exception rather than the rule. We hope this book will provide for them, but also for the more common situation of larger classes of less able, and perhaps less willing pupils too. The third assumption is that you will use only English in your lessons.

There are distinct advantages to thus using only English. Firstly, you will be confident in your use of it and can express yourself much more fluently and accurately than you will in your target language.

Secondly, if there is a misunderstanding it will be because they misunderstand, not because you have not said what you meant. Thirdly, people's comprehension of a foreign language is always greater than their ability to use it. So, when in difficulties, they are more likely to understand your fluent good English than your mistake-ridden German. From a disciplinary point of view, it is important to avoid confrontations. If they say something and they know that you have heard and understood it, you will have to respond and there is a danger of an incident developing. If you can keep a straight face and simply say, *I'm afraid I don't understand, what does that mean?* very few pupils, in our experience, are prepared to repeat something impertinent directly to you – particularly if you are smiling encouragingly at the time.

Finally, if you use only English, then everything you do is of direct value. Everything you say is a real, natural use of the language and helps your pupils to see that English is not just a subject on the timetable, but is something of real practical use.

We have lectured for the last few years to a considerable number of people who were going off to be assistants. Many have provided feedback when they returned to Britain. The most common comment of all is, *Why didn't you stress more firmly that I shouldn't use French/German/Spanish/Italian?*

When you arrive you have an in-built advantage: you're a novelty, straight from Britain, and you speak English naturally. Don't throw away that advantage by using the pupils' language in your classroom.

The main theme of our suggestions is that the activities you organise should be both conversations and lessons.

Chapter 1

Selection of teaching material

1.1 Practical criteria for choosing material

Starting a conversation from nothing is extremely difficult. Of course some local incident or something that has happened to a particular pupil will occasionally spark off a spontaneous discussion or conversation. Almost always, however, it is better to start from something concrete. This may be a text, picture, tape, anecdote told by the teacher, or whatever. The important thing is that there is some concrete focus as a basis for the conversation. You have probably already thought of using newspaper articles, pop or folk songs, maps, and pictures of the part of Britain you come from, and so on. But all too often the fascinating article from The Sunday Times that you have chosen for your class turns out to be a flop – which could have been predicted in advance. An article that interests you will often be linguistically or intellectually way beyond the ordinary pupil, and it must be obvious that your students (who may be living on a small farm outside Malaga or in the middle of the Auvergne) will have very different interests and experiences from your own.

Most assistants in the past have used the criterion 'is the subject matter interesting?' Lots of materials that pass this test for you, simply do not work in the classroom. So it is worthwhile thinking of a more comprehensive list of selection criteria.

(a) Start by considering whether the material you have in mind is practically possible in a particular situation. As soon as you arrive at your school find out, for example, if there are tape recorders and if so what kind. Find out what kind of copying facilities there are. Will you be allowed to use them? How much notice do you need to give if you want copies? Is there an overhead projector in the classroom? If so, does it have a roll of film and pens, or will you need to take your own pens? Does it have film you can take away and prepare in advance? What English newspapers and magazines does the school take? Do the other staff use them?

(b) Use this list to check the practicality of a particular idea or piece of material.

(i) Who needs the material – will you need a single copy or one for each pupil? The practical difficulties – if there are not enough (legible) copies – will overwhelm everything else.

(ii) Is the material versatile – can it be used at different levels with different groups? A simple street map is a good example. A good one for use at a basic level will have a central area with right-angled street corners to practise 'finding the way'. Away from the centre it will have a roundabout and perhaps a Y-junction so that it can be used at higher levels too (e.g. 'bear left at the traffic lights'). The map is even better if the names of different buildings are marked so that it can be used for vocabulary and perhaps even as a basis for a story (*You're standing outside the bank; what can you see, who can you see, what's he doing, where's he going?*).

We have tried to give lots of examples of well designed conversation materials that can be used with a very wide range of pupils in chapter 3.

(iii) How long will it take to present the material? If it is material only the teacher has, think of the following problems. How long will it take to write on the

board? Can you write it on the board before the class arrives? If you are going to write on the blackboard for more than, say, half a minute what are the pupils going to do while you are writing? If you do not give them something definite to do, they will almost certainly have ideas of their own!

If you are going to read to the class, how long will that take? If more than two or three minutes, how can you break up that time?

If you are going to play a tape how long will that take? Very few classes can listen to a tape (of any sort) for more than 90 seconds without a break. This of course means that you will lose the concentration of almost everybody if you play a song — they are nearly always longer than 90 seconds. If you want to avoid losing everybody's concentration you should break tapes, no matter how interesting, into short sections by, for example, asking a couple of questions or commenting yourself.

In the case of materials which the pupils also have, how long will it take them to read and understand it? How long will you spend actually using it. Materials which are to be used for conversation lessons should take a relatively short time to present so that an interesting newspaper item which takes so long to present that there is no time left to talk about it is obviously unsatisfactory. For this reason it is often better to present texts not by giving the pupils a copy but by reading extracts yourself or even preparing a summary. If the material is to be used as the basis for a conversation or discussion, it is sufficient to summarise the main ideas.

Material should be too easy rather than too difficult — difficult material invariably takes much too long to present. Many teachers forget, however, that it is very easy to increase the difficulty of simple material by adding to it. In contrast, it is very difficult indeed to simplify something that was intrinsically too difficult.

(iv) How difficult is the material? The material can be difficult for two different reasons — the language used to present it is intrinsically difficult, or the pupil does not have the background or expectations to understand it.

It is not new words or expressions which make language material difficult. It is the proportion of the whole which you do not know. This is particularly important in the case of newspapers. Quality English newspapers are written at a vocabulary level of about 20,000 words. No foreign school student has a vocabulary of even half that size. Furthermore, many words which are common in newspaper English are very uncommon in school textbooks, or in everyday spoken English. This means pupils will have considerable difficulty making any sense of most newspaper articles.

Many of the materials we suggest will be such that pupils will not know individual items or structures if they are following a traditional structural course in their schools. This does not necessarily make the lessons too difficult for them. It simply means you have to present a particular item without a complicated grammatical explanation. (The *conditional* comes quite late in a school syllabus and is regarded as a 'difficult structure' but almost anyone who learns English will want to say *I'd like some . . . please* or *Would you like to . . .?* fairly early on. Notice, though, the pupil does not need to know that he is using the conditional. You say simply 'when you ask for something, use *I'd like . . . please*'.)

Pupils will find material difficult which is outside their experience. Many of your pupils will have had very little experience outside their own families and schools. Probably very few will have had experience outside their own country, except what they may have gathered from TV, so the subjects you choose and the way you handle them should reflect this. It is not very realistic to expect them to do something in a foreign language which they would find difficult even in their own.

Finally, if you expect behaviour from the pupils which is very different from that which they are used to in school, they will find the change difficult. In particular, if they are used to sitting quietly and reading or writing and you expect them to talk a lot you will find it helpful to make that explicit.

(v) Is the material interesting? Nothing which is too difficult — which you can't understand — is interesting, so keep materials simple and within the pupils' range of experience. Here is a checklist which attempts to define more explicitly the meaning of 'interesting' in this context.

1 Will it seem useful to the pupil?
He may feel it is useful in three contexts — for an examination, practical use when, for example, visiting England, or for his other studies. (This last may require some explanation. For older pupils if you can find English articles relevant to their other lessons it can be stimulating and rewarding for them and you to use these. This is relatively straightforward for English or history. In the case of science subjects where you will not have such a detailed knowledge you may find it rewarding to use more general articles from, for example, *The Scientific American*, or *The New Scientist*.)

2 Does it stimulate the pupils' curiosity?
You will surely have watched a television programme on a subject which you were not interested in beforehand but which caught your imagination. This happens in class too, so you should not try to predict too certainly in advance what subjects pupils will find interesting. Your lively presentation of the subjects you are inter-ested in will almost certainly get them involved too.

Especially useful in this respect are puzzles. The answer itself is unimportant but, well presented, most people do enjoy solving them. In 4.6 we suggest lots of language puzzles which exploit both the intrinsic interest of language and the intellectual challenge of puzzles or problem solving.

3 Is the material relevant to the class and individual pupils?
Few school pupils in the Black Forest will be interested in the English legal system or the industries of Yorkshire. On the other hand, two people will usually be of particular interest — himself and you. For this reason you should not be afraid to talk about yourself. If asked to do lessons about, for example, the British legal system, try to do it from a personal point of view. In the same way elicit personal responses from the pupils — not from one individual but from several, or even in a small group from all the pupils.

Pupils will usually also be interested in information about themselves, their town and country as they are seen by other people. In other words, if you can find articles in English about France, or the French school system, or whatever, pupils will usually want to read these. They are curious to see how other people see them and their situation. Most importantly, what will make them most active is if the attitudes expressed in the material are surprising to them or, even better, if the factual information given is actually wrong, or prejudiced. If the pupil believes you are misinformed, he will naturally and automatically want to correct you. The interest which arises here is no longer in the subject matter but to do with his interest in you as a person. In the same way any matter upon which the pupil is better informed than you will usually stimulate him to language production. It may mean asking him about the town he lives in or getting him to explain how the tape-recorder in his classroom works. Natural conversation often depends upon an *information gap* – the participants having different information at their disposal. Traditional conversation lessons frequently fail precisely because everybody has the same information (the text). Much of the material we suggest exploits this information gap, but best of all is to exploit natural situations which actually arise in the classroom.

4 Is it fun to do?

Interest frequently derives not from what is done but from how it is done. Grammar practices of the kind you probably remember yourself ('put *du, de la* or *des* in the following sentences', followed by a seemingly endless written exercise) were usually not fun. But the sort of practices mentioned on pp. 93–4, done orally and quickly, can be entertaining and a few mistakes often make it both more useful and more fun.

5 Will it seem worth doing to the pupil?

Pupils need to see the point in doing something. This is particularly true of games. Just playing games can easily seem childish, so if you do play games show why you played the game. Explain explicitly why you did it and what they have learned or practised.

(vi) Can you handle the material?

No matter how good an idea, in the end it is you, the individual teacher, who has to handle it. A few warnings should suffice here – do NOT do anything where you are not confident of your knowledge about it. This means you should not be afraid to refuse requests like 'could you tell them a little bit about the British legal system please'. Never forget that it is not reasonable to ask you to teach what you yourself imperfectly understand.

Do NOT take material into the room before you are clear what you are going to do with it. Few materials are intrinsically interesting – they depend on you exploiting them.

The central question to help you decide how to handle a piece of material is – what *linguistic* activity will this generate?

This is so important we give a simple example. Can you think of a simple well-known game which you could play with young children which would teach them these items: please, I'd like, have got.

The answer is of course Happy Families. This is a much better conversation lesson with a class of youngsters who know very little English than a laborious effort to make them produce one or two spontaneous sentences. (Don't forget many foreigners use *have* instead of *have got*; the use of *please* is difficult for a lot of foreigners; and they are often taught to say *I want* instead of *I'd like*. So the game we've suggested is a real significant step in the right direction for a good conversation lesson.)

In summary, in the classes you give, you should try to produce not stimulating lively discussions – of course you hope for that sometimes with some of your classes – but your general objective should be a more down-to-earth one; to produce linguistic activity in the classroom by trying to make the pupils talk as much as possible in a relatively controlled way.

In the next chapter we suggest some language which is worth practising. Much of it you will think very simple but you will be surprised to find the pupils – even many who have studied English for quite a long time and know a lot of vocabulary – have considerable trouble *using* this language. Later we suggest a whole range of materials which will help to generate linguistic activity even in less able and less motivated classes. We hope you will also make your own materials but if you do, we suggest that if they are going to be easy to make, easy to use, and effective, you bear in mind the criteria discussed above.

Chapter 2

Teaching materials – 1

2.1 The sort of language you could teach

If you ask your host colleague what he expects you to do, he will probably answer 'conversation' and 'spoken English', seeing these as synonymous. However, there is a whole area that we can define as 'spoken English', which he will find difficulty in teaching, but which you are ideally suited to teach. It is the area of everyday communicative English – what to say to build normal relationships in normal situations.

In speech we show our attitudes to each other in our use of a whole set of words, phrases, and structures, eg. 'I'm sorry', 'I'm afraid', 'anyway'. The misuse of such phrases is the greatest cause of misunderstanding of foreigners. The average European learner at present is better at producing grammatically correct sentences than at producing appropriate ones. His lack of knowledge in this communicative area means that he misunderstands and that he – as a person – is misunderstood. It is not uncommon for someone who is a normal friendly person in his own language to come over as someone quite different in the foreign language, perhaps more diffident or even surly.

In teaching this area of language, it is more important than ever to remember that speaking a foreign language is very different from speaking your own. As natives we instinctively know what language is appropriate, and we can predict the effect it will have on others. Our choice of language, like dress, is also a means of expressing our personality. The teacher of language must do two things. He must explain the effect of a piece of language – what assumptions the listener will make about the speaker's age, attitudes, and personality. He must then go on to teach the kind of language which matches the age, attitudes, etc of the learner. Clearly in class you should teach the kind of language which will be most generally acceptable, and since most foreign learners use their language to relative strangers (taxi-drivers, shop assistants etc), your aim should be to present them with a slightly more formal register than you would use yourself. This has the advantage of compensating for mistakes in intonation.

Classes will find this work all the more enjoyable if you use as much of the language given in this section as often and as naturally as you can around the classroom. Never, for example, open a window yourself. Ask the class what you should say to get one of the pupils to open it for you. You will then find that pupils will look for situations to use what they have learned.

Some ideas for presentation

If you merely present the language in this section (i.e. write it on the blackboard and explain it) you have not taught it. Here is a possible sequence of activities:

1 Describe a situation:
   Someone has just stopped you in the street and said to you, 'Excuse me, could you tell me the time please?' You haven't got a watch. What do you say?
2 Comment on the responses, saying why they are appropriate/inappropriate, eg 'No, that's much too intimate/formal etc'.
3 Agree on a suitable response. Get the class repeating the phrase both in and out of context – several times.

4 Build up a simple dialogue (see method for teaching a dialogue p. 103).

5 Ask the class to translate it into their own language, and discuss the alternatives. Ask questions like:

Could your parents or grandparents say that?

Could you say that yourself?

Could I say it and sound natural?

Can I miss it out?

Can you put it at the beginning/ end of a sentence?

Does it matter if a man or a woman says it?

This final discussion helps the pupils think about the conversational phrases in their own language, which makes it easier to understand your explanations of the English ones. Above all, it makes the point that what you say has an effect on your listener. An awareness of this should lead to fewer misunderstandings.

Some important words and phrases of spoken English

Here is a list of most of the important phrases of this kind in English. We give examples of each with explicit *classroom* explanations.

1 *Thank you/thanks*

Used only for something UNimportant.

If someone does something particularly generous (something you wouldn't expect) you need to use something stronger, for example:

Thank you very much, that *was* kind of you.

Thank you, I *am* grateful.

2 *Sorry*

Used after you have inconvenienced somebody slightly.

The normal answer to 'sorry' is 'sorry'.

For something more serious we use, for example:

I *am* sorry.

I'm so sorry.

I'm terribly sorry.

often following with an explanation (I'm afraid I didn't notice it, I'm afraid I wasn't listening).

To answer a real apology like this we use:

Don't worry, that's quite all right.

3 *Sorry?/Pardon?*

Used if you would like the other person to repeat what they have said for any reason (you didn't hear/understand/believe).

'I beg your pardon' is now rather old-fashioned.

'What?' or 'What did you say?' are very informal (mostly reserved for intimate situations).

4 *Excuse me*

Used if you wish to pass somebody. (May I have your attention please, I am going to do something which may inconvenience you.)

5 *Excuse me . . .?*

Used before you ask assistance or information from somebody. (May I have your attention please, I am going to say something to you.)

Remember the basic rule in English: 'Excuse me' *before* you do something, 'Sorry' *after* you do something.

6 *Please*

This can be used in three places in spoken English:

(i) At the end of requests (the other person is going to do something for you).

Could you pass me that book please.

(ii) At the beginning of invitations (the other person is going to do something for himself).

Please don't wait for me.

Please sit down.

(iii) In the middle in situations where the speaker demands (often used as a repetition i.e. when asking for the second time).

Could you please remember to bring it tomorrow.

7 Really?

'Sorry?' is used to ask the other person to repeat the same thing. In a similar way 'really?' is used to mean 'Can you give me more details – I don't know/don't want to say anything myself just now, so would you please take the next step in the conversation?'

8 Would you?/Have you?/Are you? etc.

These are used in a similar way to 7. The auxiliary verb used is of course appropriate to the one used by the previous speaker:

A: We went up to London at the weekend.
B: Did you?

9 Yes/No

These are only used alone if it is absolutely clear to both speakers that ONLY the information in what is being said is important.

Normally such one-word answers are avoided; suitable alternatives are:

Yes please	No I'm afraid not
Yes thank you	I'm afraid we haven't/ didn't/etc.
Yes that's right	No not yet
Yes, yes we did/ have/etc.	No not quite

10 I'm afraid

This is used in all situations when giving the other person information which he may/could interpret as negative or unhelpful. In other words, it is added to semantically negative responses:

I'm afraid I haven't
I'm afraid we don't
I'm afraid we will (if this has a negative meaning to the listener)

It is easy to give an impression of unhelpfulness if you omit this when making negative responses.

11 .. really ..

When using weak or uninteresting positive adjectives we normally add really; the sentence without really will usually be interpreted negatively by the hearer.

She's a nice girl (but . .)
She's a really nice girl.

12 Not very + (a positive adjective)

It is rather rare in informal conversational English to use negative adjectives (except in 'intimate' situations). We often prefer 'not very' with the corresponding positive adjective.

It's not a very interesting job.
It wasn't very well typed.

Sentences like, 'He's short' or 'She's ugly' can sound rude and give a negative impression of the speaker of which he may be unaware.

13 Rather

In general this is often preferred in informal conversational English to very.

It was rather disappointing.
It was rather good.

It is not normally weaker than 'very'.

14 Certainly

Used to say yes in a friendly way when asked for something.

Could you change a 10p, please? Certainly.
Could you tell me the way, please? Yes, certainly.

15 Anyway

This is used to stop the present direction of a conversation. It is used:

(i) to sum up what has been said so far, very often with a view to ending the conversation, especially if it looks as if there is going to be disagreement
(ii) to stop the conversation and go back to a subject that was dropped earlier.

16 That's quite all right

This is used to accept an apology or thanks.

I'm sorry I forgot your book. Oh, that's quite all right.

Thank you very much for lending it to me. Oh, that's quite all right.

2.2 Conversational tactics

1 CONVERSATIONAL TAGS

The area of conversational tags is more misunderstood by European teachers and learners of English than almost any other area of English. It is also an area where you can put your native fluency to good use. The two most common kinds of tags are:

(a) *It's next Saturday, isn't it?*
Said with rising intonation, this is a question and needs an answer (Yes, that's right).

(b) *It's next Saturday isn't it.*
Said with a falling intonation this is *not* a question; it is an invitation to the other speaker to comment and *develop* the conversation about the topic proposed (Yes, they changed it from the 24th).

A: You've been to Italy haven't you.
B: Oh yes, we were in Rome last year at Easter.

A: You can't speak French can you.
B: Well as a matter of fact I can. I spent a year in France when I was a student.

Foreign teachers very often teach all tags as question tags, and seldom differentiate between those which *are* questions requiring an answer, and those which are conversational gambits, requiring a response.

A particularly common use of the latter is at the beginning of a conversation to talk about the weather:

Lovely day isn't it.
Yes, marvellous isn't it.

It should be clear that these ARE not and CANNOT be questions. When the foreign learner answers those tags like questions the effect can be very odd indeed:

A: You've been here before haven't you.
B: Yes, I have.
A: It's a nice place for a holiday isn't it.
B: Yes, it is.
A: And you can always depend on the weather can't you.
B: Yes, you can.

Here B is only answering: if he is a native English speaker, this means he is trying to tell A that he is not interested either in him or having a conversation with him. If B is a foreigner, does he know what he is doing? He may very well think that he is having a natural conversation.

There are endless jokes about the British talking about the weather but it is most important to realise that English has, and uses a lot, a structure which other European languages lack. It is a basic part of informal spoken English. Look at these examples:

(i) It's a dreadful morning isn't it.
(ii) You know each other don't you.
(iii) (a) You've been to Spain haven't you.
      (b) You've been to Spain haven't you?

The rules for making tags structurally are straightforward:

Positive sentences have *Negative* tags.
Negative sentences have *Positive* tags.

If the main sentence contains an auxiliary verb (or more than one) the first auxiliary is used again in the tag:

They should be able to come shouldn't they.

If there is no auxiliary verb − the sentence is either present simple or past simple − the appropriate part of do (do, does, did) is used in the tag:

They went last year didn't they.
He speaks French doesn't he.
You know them don't you.

Many sentences have two structurally identical forms but with quite different meanings, depending on intonation (see examples like (iii) above).

If the tag goes *up* at the end, the sentence is a question and of course requires an answer.

If the tag goes *down* at the end, it is a conversational invitation and requires a response.

Usually the conversational invitations are said without a pause between the main sentence and tag. Questions often have a very slight pause before the tag.

2   EXPANDING A RESPONSE

The form of tags is easily practised in the classroom. Exercises usually take the form:

Teacher: She can swim
Class: Can't she   or (Better)
Teacher: They're married
Class: They're married, aren't they

It is obvious that this is very unnatural. If this is all the teacher does the pupil does not get the idea that a tag is only the first step in a conversation. He must also learn the second step, how to respond fully.

Look at the following possible responses:

You've been to Italy haven't you?
(a) Yes
(b) Yes I have
(c) Yes I have as a matter of fact. I was there last year.
(d) Yes I have as a matter of fact – in Naples.
(e) Yes I have as a matter of fact. Have *you*?

Notice that (a) and (b) treat the statement as if it were a question. They only answer it. In a conversation they would be seen by a native speaker as 'blocking' remarks. He would assume that the other person did not wish to pursue the subject of Italy for some reason. However, the others are all natural friendly responses which make a positive contribution to the conversation. (c) and (d) tell the other person that Italy is an acceptable subject and suggest development. (e) turns the conversation back on the first person, but it leaves him in no doubt about the next move. Notice that in (e) there is a direct question. This is appropriate here, but would not have been if it had been the opening gambit of this part of the conversation.

It is by teaching conversational techniques of this kind that you can have real conversation lessons as we discussed in the opening chapter.

3   SIMPLE MANIPULATIVE RESPONSES

In natural English, Yes and No used alone are relatively rare. Much more common are responses involving the repetition of the auxiliary verb of the previous speaker, for example:

Do you know Viv?	*Does she go much?*
Yes, I do/No, I	Yes, she does/No,
don't.	she doesn't.
It's ready, isn't it.	*It's not very nice is*
Yes, it is./No (I'm	*it.*
afraid) it isn't.	No, it isn't.

Very often these short responses are followed by:

actually   or   *as a matter of fact*

It's worth pointing out to classes that the difference between a one word answer (Yes) and a fuller answer (Yes, it is actually) can make the difference between natural and unnatural English and the difference between people thinking you are a normal, friendly person or an odd and rather abrupt foreigner. In our experience the idea that language is something personal is important and, as pupils begin to understand this, it makes lessons more interesting, more relevant and more fun.

4   INTERESTED RESPONSES

We use a very similar pattern to encourage the other person to talk:

A: I've just been to London.
B: Oh, have you?
A: I took my driving test last week.
B: Oh, did you?

5   AGREEING WITH SOMEONE ELSE

Again, we use a simple manipulative response with the auxiliary verb:

A: I'd love to visit London.
B: So would I.
B: But I wouldn't like to go in the winter.
A: No, neither would I.
A: I studied French at school.
B: So did I.
A: I wasn't very good at it though.
B: No, neither was I.

6 SAYING NO IN A PLEASANT WAY

Very often the auxiliary verb is manipulated in the response:

A: *Can* you change a pound, please?
B: I'm sorry, I'm afraid I *can't*.
A: *Do* you know if there's a bank near here please?
B: I'm sorry I'm afraid I *don't*.

7 EXPRESSING YOURSELF MORE STRONGLY

One of the main ways in English of showing that there is an emotional force behind what you say is to stress the auxiliary verb. Notice, for example, the difference in these sentences:

I've been waiting quite a long time now.
I *have* been waiting quite a long time now.

There's a bank in King Street.
There *is* a bank in King Street.

I asked him as soon as I saw him.
I *did* ask him as soon as I saw him.

It's worth noticing that most European teachers are still very bound up with teaching written English, where the differences between a stressed and an unstressed verb form is of course very difficult to make. As a result, most pupils produce the full form of the verb far too often.

The above is an attempt to make a conversation lesson which actually teaches pupils how a conversation can be constructed. Notice how concrete these materials are compared to traditional 'what-would-you-like-to-talk-about?' lessons. Try it with a group and see if they *enjoy* a lesson which is concrete and, in fact, rather grammatically based. You may be surprised!

2.3 The importance of the auxiliary in English

Natural spoken English usually reduces auxiliary verbs. We only stress them if there is a special (emotional) force behind what we're saying. This is an important difference to learn for pupils who are a little more advanced. It is important for them to be able to express both their emotions and the basic ideas. Stress patterns are very important for showing emotion and are usually ignored by their own teachers.

There are a number of other common conversational patterns which are based on the manipulation of the verb – particularly the auxiliary verb. Notice that in all the examples above, the ability to hear and manipulate the auxiliary verb is central to being able to use the language fluently. Unfortunately, schools which still do a good deal of traditional grammar teaching produce pupils who know how to make such sentences, but who do not realise how important they are in natural, spoken English. You can help a lot by encouraging them to practise.

There is an important grammatical rule of English with which you may not be familiar, and which is shown by the patterns above. A great many patterns of English depend on manipulating the auxiliary verb. It is a completely general rule that if a pattern needs an auxiliary verb and there is no auxiliary in the particular sentence part of the verb, (do) is used instead:

I've met him before.	I know him quite well.
Oh, have you.	*Oh, do you.*
I've been here half an hour.	I asked 20 minutes ago.
I have been here half an hour.	*I did ask 20 minutes ago.*

This also applies to making questions and negatives in English:

He's coming.
Is he coming?

He knows her.
Does he know her?

She was there yesterday.
She wasn't there yesterday.

She saw him yesterday.
She didn't see him yesterday.

Remember, it's an absolutely general rule that part of (do) is used as a 'dummy auxiliary' if the structural or stress pattern needs an auxiliary and the particular positive sentence doesn't contain one; i.e. it is in the present simple or past simple. This regularity of English is often not pointed out to pupils and, indeed, many foreign teachers do not even see it as a regular pattern. You may be able to help by pointing it out.

2.4   Functions of English

The following is a list of some of the most important functions a foreigner might need when speaking English. Some of the most important language necessary to perform each function is given. The commentary shows you the teaching points − the areas that foreigners often find difficult. We hope this will help you to make your own little dialogues.

LANGUAGE

1 Starting a conversation
Oh hello, how are you?
Fine thanks, and you?
Very well, thank you.
Lovely day, isn't it.
Yes, beautiful, isn't it.

2 Introducing people
Mary, this is John. He works/lives . . .
John, this is Mary. She . . .
Mary, I'd like you to meet John.
How do you do.
Pleased to meet you.

3 Inviting people
Would you like to . . .
I wonder if you'd like to . . .
Yes, that'd be lovely.
Oh, I'd love to, but I'm afraid I . . .

4 Making suggestions
What about . . .ing,
Why not . . .
Why don't you . . .
That's a good idea.

5 Making a plan together
Shall we . . .
Why don't we . . .
Wouldn't it be a good idea if we . . .
Yes, what a good idea. Why don't we!

COMMENTARY

1.
Notice particularly: the word order/tags.
When we agree we normally use a different word with the same meaning (lovely, beautiful).

2.
There are lots of different things here depending on the degree of formality.

3.
Remember as a general principle, anything that involves an offer/request/enquiry etc. has two different possible answers, the positive and the negative.

4.
This and the next example − apart from positive/negative answers, students also need the language to agree/disagree partially and to suggest alternatives.

6 Asking for help

Excuse me, could you . . . please.
          would you . . . please.
          could you possibly . . .
            please.

6.

Differences of age and background are important in this one. It uses a lot of grammatically difficult constructions which should be explained by *why* we use them (when we want to ask for help we say . . .) and not grammatically.

7 Apologising about something (which is not very serious, but you think is your fault)

I'm so sorry
I am sorry
Don't worry that's quite all right.

7.

Notice the difference between these and a casual *sorry* (often answered *sorry*). These examples contain one stressed word between *I* and *sorry*.

8 Asking for, giving and refusing permission

May I . . .
Do you mind if I (open the window)
Would you mind if I (open<u>ed</u> the window)
Certainly (the answer to May I . . .)
No, please do ⎱ (answers to Do/would you
No, not at all ⎰ mind/if . . .)
I'd rather you didn't (+ an excuse)
I'd prefer you not to (+ an excuse)

8.

This is one of the most difficult. The answers require relatively difficult grammar and a good deal of imagination for excuses.

9 Showing interest and enthusiasm

Really? (Did) you?/(Can) you?
What + uncountable noun
(What lovely furniture!)
What a + singular noun
(What a lovely dress!)

9.

Intonation is important. For this reason it can be good fun with a class, although the grammar (countable and uncountable nouns) is quite difficult.

10 Asking for and giving advice

What do you think (I should do)?
Do you think it's a good idea?
Well, it depends.
Well, it's difficult to say.
Why don't you . . .
If I were you I'd . . .
Have you thought of . . .ing.
That's an excellent idea, thanks very much.
Yes, but don't forget . . .

10.

This is very dependent on who is talking to whom, how old they are, how well they know each other etc.

11 Showing that you're annoyed (in a restaurant or shop)

I'm sorry, I *did* ask for . . .
I'm sorry, I *have* been waiting for 15 minutes.
I *would* like . . . now.
I'm sorry, this just isn't good enough.
I'm sorry, I'm afraid I'm annoyed now. This has gone a little too far.
Could I speak to the manager/the person in charge, please.

11.

The basic rule here is that when we are annoyed we stress a word which is not normally stressed. The phrases at the end are, of course, very strong and may sound odd from a foreigner. They should certainly only be taught to advanced pupils.

12 Agreeing and disagreeing about something (less serious)

What did you think of . . . I thought it
  was . . .
So (did) I. That's exactly what I thought
  myself.
Well, actually, I thought it was
  rather ⎫
  a bit ⎬ + (negative adjective)
Umm, do you really think so.
Well, no as a matter of fact I (didn't).
Oh well, I don't suppose it matters very
  much anyway.

12.
This and the next one are difficult, but
  very important. Remember that disagree-
  ing is always more difficult than agreeing.
  Notice especially:
    So (. . .) I
    Neither (. . .) I
  as a very common tactic for agreeing.
  See p. 70ff for further practice.

13 Agreeing and disagreeing about something (more serious)

There I agree with you completely.
I wouldn't go as far as to say that, but I
  think . . .
I think that's going a bit too far. After all,
  what about . . .
I see your point, but are you sure . . .
I can't entirely agree there I'm afraid. I
  think . . .
Oh I really can't/couldn't agree with that.

14 Asking for and giving directions

Excuse me, I wonder if you could tell me if
  there's a (bank) near here, please.
Excuse me, could you tell me where the
  Theatre Royal is, please?
I'm sorry, I'm afraid I'm a stranger here
  myself.
Go straight along   Go down/up   Turn
  left/right
Take the first/second/third on your left/
  right.
It's on the left/right beside   next to
  opposite   between   across from
  go past   on the corner   bear right/left
Thank you very much.
Not at all. You can't miss it.

14.
Remember, in this case it's often very
  important for the pupils to be able to
  understand instructions given by a native
  speaker. Give them a map, let them ask
  you for places and then give the answers
  quickly in the sort of muddled language
  people often use. Of course, you can also
  use the map more conventionally.

15 Asking for and offering things

Could I have a . . . please?
I'd like a . . . please.
Would you like a . . . ?
Have you any/a . . . please?
Yes, please/No thank you.

16 Using the telephone

(a) A private phone call
Oh, hello. Is . . . there please?
Oh, hello. Can I speak to . . . please?
Just a moment, please.
Can/could I/you take/leave a message
  please?
I'll ring/call back.

16(a).
Remember how we give numbers in
  English:
7730 – Double seven three oh.
The difference between can/could/may is
  important here.
Language on the telephone is very stereotyped. It's easy to write standard
  dialogues but remember to add some
  noises like *'Oh'*, too).

(b) A business call
Good morning, extension six please.
I'm afraid it's engaged at the moment.
  Would you like to hold on?
No thank you. I'll call back later.
Perhaps you could ask . . . to ring me back.
  Thank you. Goodbye.

16(b).
This should only be done with older pupils.

17 Breaking a conversation and keeping in touch

(a) In someone's home
Just look at the time. I'd no idea it was so
  late. I really must be going now I'm
  afraid.
I really must go, I'm afraid.
I'll really have to go/be going, I'm afraid.
It's been a lovely evening, thank you very
  much.
Give my regards to . . .
Remember me to . . .

17(a).
Remember, it's normal in Britain to say
  you're going to leave *twice*, using two
  different phrases.

(b) In the street
I'll have to be going now, I'm afraid.
Sorry I can't stop.
See you later. See you again.
Bye bye. Cheerio.

17(b).
Collect and discuss different expressions
  meaning *Goodbye*.

18 Expressing sympathy

Oh, how dreadful/terrible/awful
What a terrible shock/what an awful thing
  to happen.
I am/so/terribly sorry to hear that.
Well, these things happen, don't they.
Well, things like this happen, don't they.

18.
This is very difficult to do naturally, but it
  is useful in case pupils ever need it. The
  phrases are rather stereotyped.

2.5 Situations

Here is a list of very specific situations where a learner can practise and learn the special language used in that particular situation. This list should suggest dialogue which you can write yourself.

1 At the railway station – buying a ticket.
2 At the garage – buying petrol.
3 At the doctor's.
4 At the dentist's.
5 At the barber's/hairdresser's.
6 In the restaurant/coffee bar/refreshment counter.
7 In the post office – buying stamps/sending a telegram.
8 In the bank or bureau de change.
9 At the theatre/cinema/booking office.
10 Shopping; for example, buying a film, buying a shirt, etc.
11 At the chemist's – buying something, or explaining 'what's wrong'.

Pupils, particularly younger ones, will find nearly all of the situations more fun and more realistic if you've taken with you something – a ticket, a timetable, a menu, or whatever – that is real. In chapter 5 we suggest some of the things that you might take with you to help out in this sort of lesson.

Chapter 3

Teaching Materials — 2

3.1 The first lesson

The most important aim in a first lesson is for you to come over as a real person. This means deciding what you are going to do before you go in, then going in (preferably with no material) and *looking at* the pupils. As soon as you take your eyes off them you lose contact, and if you do not come across as a person they will lose interest and may not come back. Your main aim should be to make them want to come back to your next session.

1 Start the class by introducing yourself — by talking for five minutes about yourself. Then ask them questions about what you have told them. You will soon find out how well they have understood you.

2 Make the class active. Many classes will not be used to speaking English and if you can make them speak to each other at your first lesson, they will be all the more positive to you. Put some questions on the board and get the pupils to interview each other in pairs.

Here are some sample questions:

Which part of the town do you live in?
What are you interested in outside school?
What do you like to do at the weekends?
Have you ever been to England?
Have you ever spoken to any other Englishman?

Walk around all the time listening and making sure that they are speaking English. Make it clear when you want them to stop (clap once loudly!) then get some of them to report what they have found out about their friend.

3 Make it clear to the class that English will be the only language you allow in the room. Then teach the class something obviously useful that they do not already know; for example, teach (at any level) what to say to you the next time they see you:

> Hello, how are you.
> *Fine thanks, and you.*
> Very well, thank you.

(Pupils always find this 'ritual greeting' difficult.)

End the lesson with a short language game for five or ten minutes (see p. 34ff). Do not expect to do too much in this first lesson — if they have heard you, understood some of your English, spoken a few sentences themselves and above all enjoyed the class, you have started out properly and effectively.

3.2 Lesson introductions

A lesson that starts:

> Right everyone, turn to page 76.
> *or* Today I'm going to teach you . . .

is a very dreary and unnatural activity, and does not give the class time to adjust to English. More importantly the class cannot see *why* they should be turning to page 76 or why they need to learn what you have decided to present. So, you need to talk a little to give them some time to get used to spoken English again, and they need to be given some motivation.

1 The simplest of all introductions is to greet the whole class or individuals with,

> Hello, how are you today?

With a young class don't be afraid to have them all shout back,

> Very well, Miss Macleod, and how are you?

With an older class greet individuals in the same way. Many otherwise competent students cannot handle a simple natural greeting.

2 A simple introduction to teach *I'm afraid* would be:

> I've just been speaking to a friend of mine who lives here. I asked him if he would like to come round to my place this evening for a cup of tea and a chat. He can't come because he always goes to football training on Thursdays. What do you think he said to me when he said 'No'?

This accustoms the class to English (Don't forget that they've probably just come from Maths), and they can see the usefulness more directly than if you had said, 'Well, today we're going to learn about *I'm afraid*'.

3 The above kind of concrete introduction is even more crucial for discussion lessons. To walk into a room and announce that today 'we're going to talk about capital punishment', is a recipe for failure. A more natural introduction is:

> Good morning everybody, I've just got a long letter from my grandmother. She lives alone, you know, so she likes writing to me. She was saying that a man in the next street murdered his wife and two children – just poisoned them all one evening at supper. He put something in the teapot. And they're sending him to prison for life. She thinks this is terrible. She says that all her friends, and she agrees with them, think he should be hanged. What do you think? Is she right?

Notice that this lesson needed no elaborate stencils or machinery. The only thing you need is a page of your grandmother's letter (which of course you can write the night before if necessary). The basic way to introduce a lesson, then, is to begin with a natural greeting – either to the whole class or to individuals (and to insist on a response) then:

1 When introducing a language point – present the class with a situation where the language is needed and ask the class, 'What do you think he said when . . .?'

2 When introducing ideas for discussion, be as concrete and realistic as possible. Start from a situation rather than an abstract question. If the matter is contentious in any way and you want to avoid expressing your view, at least at this early stage, use the technique mentioned above – attribute a decisive discussable view to a third person whom you have met, got a letter from, or whatever.

3.3   Speech work

The following phonetic symbols are used in this section:

/ ə /   as in auth*or*, col*our*, furni*ture*
/i/   as in s*i*t
/i:/   as in s*ea*t
/ æ /   as in s*a*t
/ ʌ /   as in s*u*ch
/ θ /   as in *th*ink
/ ð /   as in *th*ere
/ ʃ /   as in *sh*ip, *s*ugar, na*t*ion
/ ʒ /   as in plea*s*ure, *G*iscard
/ ʧ /   as in *ch*urch
/z/   as in the*s*e, *z*oo, Su*s*an
/j/   as in *y*ellow, huge/hju:/
/ ʤ /   as in *G*erman, ma*j*or

The other letters have their normal English values (p, b, v etc.)

Even if you will not normally be required to 'teach' pronunciation, you will be expected to correct errors and help individuals with particular problems. Five minutes pronunciation work at any one time is enough. Pronunciation teaching can be of very doubtful value since very often, at least for older pupils, the only way to get rid of bad habits is to work for a long time with individual pupils in language laboratories. Few teachers have the time or the facilities for this kind of work. Nevertheless, classes very often feel that pronunciation exercises are useful and fun. They are also very useful as a means of control, since they involve the whole group doing the same thing at the same time.

You can do pronunciation practice:

(i)   When someone makes a mistake which you recognise as relatively common (and therefore worth the attention of the whole group).

(ii) When you decide to have a change of activity or pace for five minutes in the middle of the lesson.

(iii) At the end as a filler to give some practice on a common problem.

CORRECTING A PRONUNCIATION MISTAKE

Notice how little language the teacher uses in this correction transcript:

T: What did you do yesterday?
P: I went to ze seatre.
T: No, not ze seatre. Listen . . . the theatre . . . the . . . the. Say after me: the.
P: Ze.
T: No, listen again . . . the . . . / ð / . . . say it.
P: Ze.
T: No, listen . . . the . . . When you say ze your tongue is behind your top teeth. Feel it.
P: Ze.
T: When I say the, the end of my tongue is below my top teeth. Look. (Teacher comes closer and shows pupil his tongue below his top teeth in the correct position.) Now listen again . . . / ð / . . . / ð /.
P: / ð /.
T: Good. Now say, the theatre.

Notice some of the basic techniques:

1 The basic method is repetition − say after me.
2 Keep your language to the minimum − it helps to use imperatives: Listen; say it; listen, not ze, the.
3 Isolate the problem for the pupil − not seatre, theatre. Contrast clearly what is wrong with what is correct.
4 If an explanation is required keep it simple − avoid phonetic terms. As far as possible demonstrate the sound yourself.
5 When the pupil shows improvement encour-age him − even if it's only partly right. Don't expect sudden permanent improvement.
6 Remember if you pick on someone's pronunciation he can easily get embarrassed. If one person makes a mistake correct him. If he shows signs of embarrassment, involve the whole class and get everyone to have a go.

DOING A PRONUNCIATION PRACTICE

It is very easy to make your own materials for pronunciation practice. Make a list of all the sounds of English which your students will find difficulty with − you will find some help with this below. Then write some short phrases containing the sound.

For example, if pupils find the difference between /s/ and / ʃ / difficult, they will find the following phrases a problem:

> *She's sure*
> *Simon's shirt*
> *Show Sue your new silk shirt*

They are not 'tongue twisters' in the normal sense. To use them:

1 Say them clearly yourself.
2 Write on blackboard.
3 Get the whole class to repeat them after you.
4 Ask individual pupils to say them.

This is a light-hearted way to check up on pronunciation, and a fun thing to do for the last five minutes of a lesson.

TEACHING PUPILS TO 'HEAR' DIFFERENT SOUNDS

One of the reasons that pupils sometimes cannot make a sound is that they cannot 'hear' the difference between that sound and a similar one in their own language. A very simple technique for checking this, using *minimal pairs*, consists of presenting the pupil with two words which are the same except for the one sound the pupil is having trouble with, for example:

ship sip – the difference between / ʃ / and /s/

three tree – the difference between / θ / and /t/

The method is as follows:

1   Write the two words on the blackboard.
2   Beside the first write *1* and beside the other *2*.
3   Say to the pupil(s), 'When I say this one (pointing) you say *1* and when I say that one you say *2*'.
4   Say the words several times, varying the word you say, and checking if they are identifying them correctly. Do the same thing again but with your back to the class, so that they cannot see your lips.

If the pupils get this right, then they can obviously hear the difference. If not, you must go back and do the minimal pair exercise again, slowly and showing them the difference as clearly as possible.

Minimal pairs can also be used for production – if you can find several pairs with the same difference ask individual pupils in the group to say a pair after you, but do remember they will find this difficult. Remember, too, that you should not normally spend more than five minutes at any one time on a pronunciation problem.

Pronunciation is popular and useful for younger children. They often have a good ability to mimic until about 13-years-old. For older pupils, however, bad pronunciation is often an ingrained habit and something of an embarrassment.

If you have a number of pupils with a lot of serious problems, mention it to their ordinary teachers. It may help both the teachers and pupils and be interesting for you if you could spend some time working individually with these problem pupils.

Here is a list of the main problem sounds with some minimal pairs and 'tongue twister phrases' for native speakers of French, German, Spanish and Italian.

THE MAIN PROBLEMS FOR FRENCH SPEAKERS

Each syllable in French has approximately the same length and stress. French rhythm is based on an equal number of stresses in each time unit. English rhythm is based on an equal number of stressed *syllables* in each time unit. To achieve this, English reduces a great many intervening syllables. Many English structural words (auxiliary verbs, pronouns, etc.) are most often produced with weak forms. These do not exist in French and cause considerable problems since pupils usually overproduce. This means that / ə / is usually replaced by other vowels according to the spelling.

The main phonetic difficulties are as follows:
/i/ and /i:/ are confused. Usually /i:/ is used for both.
/ æ / and / ʌ / are confused. / ʌ / is usually used for both.
The /r/ sound in French is different from its English equivalent.
/h/ does not occur in French and is often omitted in English ('e's been on 'is 'olidays).
/ θ / and / ð / do not occur in French and are usually replaced by /s/ and /z/.

THE MAIN PROBLEMS FOR SPANISH SPEAKERS

Rhythm in Spanish is like that of French. Usually each syllable has approximately the same length, and the grouping of syllables which occurs in English does not normally occur in Spanish. This means Spanish students usually have problems with the weak forms of unstressed words and the use of / ə / in weak syllables. / ə / is usually replaced by another vowel suggested by the spelling (with the addition of /r/ if the spelling has an r).

Spanish has no distinction between long and short vowels, the Spanish vowels corresponding most closely to English short vowels. This makes the English long vowels a problem for the Spanish learner. In addition, the following phonetic problems are common:

/b/ and /v/ are often confused. Spaniards usually prefer /b/.

/ ð / and /d/ are confused.

/s/ and /z/ are confused, the Spanish pupil usually using /s/ in all cases.

/ ʃ / and / ʒ / do not occur in Spanish. Both are usually replaced by /s/.

/ ʤ / and / ʧ / are usually confused, / ʧ / being used for both.

/ ʃ / is sometimes pronounced as / ʧ /.

Clusters of consonants are rare in Spanish. This means that, like Italians, Spanish pupils have a tendency to insert a vowel sound between consonant pairs either when they occur within a word, or between two words when the first terminates with a consonant sound and the second starts with a consonant sound ('Scusa me).

THE MAIN PROBLEMS FOR ITALIAN SPEAKERS

In the same way as French and Spanish students, Italian students find weak forms of unstressed words or weak syllables, usually containing / ə / in English, difficult as such forms tend not to occur in Italian.

Almost all Italian words end in vowels. This results in a tendency to pronounce a written vowel (in words like hide, made) or to add a redundant vowel (he's gota the letta).

Italian combinations of vowels tend always to be given their full value. As a result, Italian students find English dipthongs difficult.

The following sounds, which do not occur in Italian, are likely to cause problems:

/ θ / and / ð / – they are more likely to produce /t/ and /d/.

/w/ – although an approximation to this sound occurs in Italian, students often prefer to produce /v/.

/h/ – this is always silent in Italian.

/r/ – this is trilled much more emphatically in Italian.

/ ʒ / – does not occur and will need to be practised.

THE MAIN PROBLEMS FOR GERMAN SPEAKERS

The difficulties for German speakers, in contrast to speakers of Romance languages, are less likely to be concerned with stress. Their main problems will be phonetic and are as follows:

/ θ / and / ð / do not occur in German. German speakers usually replace them by /s/ and /z/.

/ ʒ / and / ʤ / do not occur (except in borrowed words) in German. They are usually replaced by / ʃ / and / ʧ /.

/w/ and /v/ are confused, /v/ being used for both. This is often a reading rather than a pronunciation problem, but attention still needs to be given to it.

/ ə / is usually over-pronounced. At the end of a word it is usually too like the English / ɔ /, elsewhere in a word too close to the English /i/.

PRACTICE MATERIAL

1 / ʤ /

Key words: *jacket, dangerous, large* (initial, medial, terminal positions)

Words: jacket – jump – job – joke – German – January – age – change – damaged – passenger

Contrast with / ʧ /
cheap – jeep, chain – Jane, choice – Joyce, cheered – jeered, choke – joke, rich – ridge, chairman – German

Contrast with /j/
jet – yet, jot – yacht, jaw – your

Phrases
In June and July
Not just yet
George is changing his job again
Jack's job makes Charles jealous
You must be joking!
Which job would you choose?

Articulation practices
I like marmalade
(enjoy – jam – John)

Cherry is going to China in March
(June – John – Germany)

Charles's starting his job in July
(John – changing – June)

The French officer had a big car
(large – general – German)

Jill had to change planes in Manchester
(Geneva – the children – jets)

The talk was jeered by the French workers
(speech – cheered – German – teachers)

See section 3.4 for how to use these articulation (fluency) practices.

2 / ʃ /
Key words: ship, station, Spanish
Words: shirt – shoes – sugar – sure – should – delicious – machine – demonstration – French

Contrast with / tʃ /
sheep – cheap, shoes – choose, shop – chop, wash – watch, wish – witch, cash – catch

Contrast with /s/
see – she, seats – sheets, save – shave, fasten – fashion, puss – push

Phrases
Fish and chips
Fashions change
Sugar's cheap
I'm sure she's the French tennis champion
Some delicious Swiss chocolate
Is this the switch?
I was so sure those were Sue's shoes
That sort of person is never ashamed so she needs a short, sharp shock

Articulation practices
He bought an expensive car
(cheap – chose – Charles)

This shop sells special food
(butcher – cheap – chops)

She saw the boys running after the dog
(chase – children – watch)

Sam got to the station before Sue
(beach – reached – Charles)

Sarah's so funny when she speaks French
(Shirley – Swedish – shy)

3 / ʒ /
This sound is relatively rare but many European foreigners do have trouble with it. It is not practical to list in the way we have listed the other sounds. Here is a list of the most common words containing this sound:

usual, pleasure, measure, leisure, casual, garage, television
Other words for more advanced classes are:

Division, revision, collision, invasion, vision, inclusion, illusion, explosion

Phrases
Casual clothes are usually worn for leisure
Leisure time is usually used for pleasure
We usually dress casually at the weekends
People watch a lot of television in their leisure time
It'll be a real pleasure to change into something casual

Articulation practices
I normally wear formal clothes for business
(casual – usually – pleasure)

4 / θ /
Key words: thank you, method, month
Words: think – theatre – thirsty – Thursday – nothing – birthday – author – bath – south – growth

Contrast with /t/
thin – tin, three – tree, thanks – tanks, thought – taught

Contrast with /f/
three – free, thirst – first, thought – fought, thrill – frill

Contrast with /s/
think – sink, thick – sick, thought – sought, thumb – some, theme – seem, teeth – tease, forth – force, worth – worse

Phrases
North and south
Thirty-three
Six months
I think Thursday's the third this year
There were between thirty and forty there
I think I'll get them something for their birthdays
Through thick and thin
They fought to be free
They're thought to be free

Articulation practices
She has two showers a week
(baths − three − month)

Ethel had a swim on Tuesday
(Judith − bath − Thursday)

He said he'd go to the cinema
(theatre − thought − Mr Smith)

5 / ð /
Key words: *then, father, with*
Words:
This sound is common as the initial sound of a number of important English structure words. These are:
the, this, that, these, those, their, they, there, then, though
   It also occurs in the middle and at the end of a number of other common words. Here are some of the most important:
either, father, another, together, rather, rhythm, smooth
(Note: Most English speakers talking naturally pronounce *clothes* as /klouz/, ie the / ð / is dropped)

Contrast with /d/
they − day, there − dare, those − doze

Contrast with /s/ or /z/
though − sew, they − say, that − sat, these − seize, breathe − breeze

Phrases
This and that
Then and there
They're over there
That's the brother

This is theirs
My mother, father and brother were there

Articulation practices
Brown's is the best café in the eastern region
(that's − bathing place − southern)

He went to Spain yesterday
(they − there − then)

There's a very nice plastic one there
(another − rather − leather)

Here are some examples which combine / θ / and / ð /.

He said the situation would get worse
(they − thought − weather)

We speak like that here
(think − there − they)

This is for my brother's party
(birthday − father − that)

6 /z/
Key words: *zoo, lazy, please*
Words: zip − easy − busy − noisy − husband − noise − cause
   Notice this sound is common in a number of important structural words:
is, isn't, does, these, those, his, hers, theirs, as, has
   It is also needed for the pronunciation of plurals (see below)

Contrast with /s/
pens − pence, prize − price, plays − place, knees − niece, peas − piece, please − police

Phrases
He's lazy
The summer season
It wasn't hers
His shoes
It's theirs, not yours
Whose shoes are those?
Socialism is based on optimism

Articulation practices
I'm annoyed by silly children
(lazy − teachers − pupils)

He has lots of property
(owns – houses – hundreds)

We gave Mary some flowers
(roses – a dozen – Susan)

7 /h/

Key words: *hat, behind* (does not occur finally)
This is mostly a problem in the initial position. Words with /h/ in the middle are relatively uncommon.

Words: half – hand – head – hear – heavy – high – home – horse – house – hundred – behind – anyhow – rehearse – perhaps – unhappy

Contrast initial /h/ and unaspirated equivalent
hand – and, hear – ear, hold – old, high – I, hair – air, hill – ill, heart – art

Phrases
He's unhappy
Awfully heavy
We all hurried home
I asked her how she heard
How awful, how did it happen?

(Notice it is normal for educated speakers to drop the /h/ and elide the word with the previous word, providing it is an unstressed structural word. This is not regarded as wrong and, while teaching pupils to aspirate words like hand, head, hotel, they must be taught at the same time to make elisions in phrases like *He must've had his hair cut*, or *It's not his own*.)

Articulation practices
John had a wonderful trip
(Harry – awful – holiday)

He was the most popular person in the film
(actor – handsome – Hollywood)

8 /p/

Key words: *pen, paper, map*
Words: page – part – people – perhaps – April – complete – happen – important – keep – help – chop

Contrast with /b/
pig – big, peach – beach, path – bath, pair – bear, pat – bat, pump – bump, tap – tab, pup – pub, repel – rebel, simple – symbol

Contrast with /v/
boat – vote, best – vest, bet – vet, ban – van, fibre – fiver, marble – marvel

Phrases
A baby puppy
Picture postcard
A big plate of soup
Apple pie
A stamped addressed envelope
They bought the baby a very expensive birthday present

Articulation practices
Barbara sat on the bench near the beach
(park – Peter – slept)

A small packet of peanuts please
(big – bananas – bunch)

9 /w/

Key words: *window, sandwich* (does not occur finally)
Words:
This sound is common at the beginning of a number of important structural words:
when – which – what – why – were – where – was – one – well – will – with
Here are some more words:
whether – watch – wonderful – water – way – woman – always – between – question – twelve – twenty – twice – everywhere – quiet

Contrast with /v/
wet – vet, wire – via, west – vest, wine – vine, wheel – veal, worse – verse, wail – vale

Phrases
Very well, thank you
Oh very well, thank you
A wonderful view over the water
World War One
We're having a holiday in November
Why are you going away in winter?

We always go to warmer weather in winter
Well, will the weather be very warm then?

Articulation practices
They had terrible trouble
(weather – we – wonderful)

They were asking where it happened
(wonder – when – we)

There's a marvellous view of the lake from our garden
(water – window – wonderful)

10 /i/
Key words: sit
Words: ill – film – minute – beginning – interesting – fifty – recipe – publicity

Contrast between /i/ and /i:/
ship – sheep, it – eat, sit – seat, his – he's, filled – field, pitch – peach, bitten – beaten

Phrases
Fifty minutes
At the beginning of the film
If he's ill he needs some pills
A cheap tin of peas
He hit the dog that bit him with a stick
I hope you're not being greedy, filling it so full!

Regular Plurals
Most English words make their plural form by adding an *s* to the spelling, but three pronunciations are possible:

After a voiceless sound, /s/ – books, hats
After a voiced sound, /z/ – plays, bottles
After the following /ʃ, s, z, ʒ, tʃ, dʒ/, /iz/– buses, garages

Third person forms in the present simple
The same rules apply here. There are three pronunciations of the *s* depending not upon the preceding letter but upon the preceding *sound:*
walks, plays, rushes

Regular past tense forms (. . .ed)
Again, although the spelling is consistent there are three different pronunciations:

After a voiceless sound /t/ – smoked, watched
After a voiced sound /d/ – slowed, opened
After /t/, /d/ or /id/ – visited, handed

Here is a list of regular verbs. You may want to use it to help pupils practise the three different pronunciations of . . .ed.

annoyed	guessed	worked	slowed
liked	listened	decided	cleaned
ruined	suggested	visited	missed
suited	booked	opened	looked
cooked	shouted	smoked	knocked
sounded	closed	handed	phoned
smiled	pulled	enjoyed	waited
hated	raced	remembered	called
danced	baked	passed	played
needed	allowed	wanted	laughed

Remember, when you are doing simple drills with pupils which involve them making plural forms or third person singular (present) forms they may have trouble with the three pronunciations of the *s*. If so, explain and then get them to practise making the regular forms in the same way as you can do with these past tense forms.

Vowel sounds
The most common vowel sound in English is / ə /. Most European learners over-pronounce it, usually using the obvious vowel from the spelling. It can replace many different letters or groups of letters.

alarm	pict*ur*e	sal*a*d	m*a*chine
ann*oy*	long*er*	p*o*lite	t*o*mato
*o*bey	op*er*a	p*er*haps	terr*i*ble
*o*ffence	sulph*ur*	ban*a*na	pil*o*t
doct*or*	coll*ar*	am*a*teur	glamor*ou*s
col*our*	chauff*eur*	condit*i*on	courag*eou*s

Pupils must be encouraged to say words naturally and to reduce the vowel to / ə /.

Stress
There are a large number of structural words in English that have (at least) two forms – one strong and one weak. The use of weak forms is an essential part of English, and English spoken only with the full strong forms sounds strange or even wrong.

You should look for the following words that may be given their strong form mistakenly. Encourage pupils to produce weak forms whenever they are speaking. (But remember, many teachers will concentrate on written English, either implicitly or explicitly, and may themselves over-produce these words. Care must of course be taken not to upset host colleagues, but it is important that students realise that the weak forms are correct, not lazy or uneducated.)

Here are the words normally reduced by educated native speakers when unstressed:

and	his	are	can	at
as	her	be	shall	for
but	them	is	will	from
than	us	was	a	of
that	do	has	an	to
he	does	have	the	not
him	am	had	some	

Here are some phrases and sentences that contain a lot of reduced words. Use one or two of the phrases from time to time to remind pupils how important the / ə / sound and the weak forms of the structural words are.

In a week or two
John and George
As soon as possible
It's old but I like it
When could we come?

How nice, we'd love to
What was that?
That'll be all, thank you
Who am I speaking to, please?
Where are we going?

I come from London
He gave her some
He's left his hat
Did you tell me?
Shall we ask him to help?

Here are some longer sentences:

At least it wasn't as bad as he'd thought
He's just been to the dentist's and had his teeth out
Of course I could've done it, if I'd had to
Does he want to give her some of them?
Shall I take her to the hospital? Or do you want to?
You must do what the doctor says or you'll get worse

Even Stress

Certain phrases, particularly initials and phrases like *boy scout* where the two-word phrase is made of words which can stand independently, usually take an even, regular stress. Here are some practice materials.

Initials

1 ABC	6 UN	11 GMT	16 PR
2 BBC	7 TV	12 ICI	17 VIP
3 SAS	8 CIA	13 KLM	18 TUC
4 IRA	9 CBI	14 USA	19 MP
5 IBM	10 FBI	15 USSR	20 RIP

(These can obviously be used in *two* ways – ask pupils to say them and to explain their meaning.)

Phrases
Say the following phrases, and stress all the words:

New Year	front room	bathroom door	First World War
Boy scout	outside	lefthand drive	Second World War
Red Cross	secondhand	ballpoint pen	

Now say these phrases:

TV show   BBC TV show   The BBC New Year TV show
The BBC New Year TV show was very bad
The BBC Tom Jones New Year TV show was very bad

Sports car   Secondhand sports car
My boyfriend has just bought a secondhand sports car
My boyfriend has just bought a lefthand-drive secondhand sports car

Part-time job   I'm thinking of taking on a part-time job
I'm getting a part-time job at weekends in the New Year

Numbers

The main difference between 13 and 30 or 15 and 50, is that in the -teen words the second syllable is not reduced, whereas it is in the -ty words.

Say these pairs: Fourteen — forty, seventeen — seventy, fifteen — fifty, thirteen — thirty.

Emphasis

We often stress a particular word to correct what someone else thinks or says or to emphasise it for some other reason. Practise saying these sentences with a strong stress on the word in capitals:

1 (a)   I expect to arrive about SEVEN o'clock
  (b)   *I* expect to arrive about seven o'clock
  (c)   I EXPECT to arrive about seven o'clock
2 (a)   My husband's going to a CONFERENCE next weekend
  (b)   My husband's going to a conference NEXT weekend
  (c)   My HUSBAND's going to a conference next weekend
3 (a)   There are TOO many foreign tourists in London in the summer
  (b)   There are too many FOREIGN tourists in London in the summer
  (c)   There are too many foreign tourists in LONDON in the summer
  (d)   There are too many foreign tourists in London in the SUMMER

Questions

In questions, stress often marks what particular piece of information is of interest to the questioner. It may also show some surprise. Try stressing the italicized words in this sentence (one at a time!):

Are *you* going to *fly* to the *conference* on *Thursday*?

Now form different questions by changing the stress on these questions so that you will get the answers given:

1 Is John going to Germany in June?
   (a) No, George is
   (b) No, he's going to Switzerland
   (c) No, he's going in July

2 Is Charles going to be chairman of the meeting on Tuesday?

   (a) No, he's going to be the secretary
   (b) No, he's going to be chairman on Thursday
   (c) No, James is

3 Did Richard take the children to the pictures?
   (a) No, he went alone
   (b) No, Charles did
   (c) No, he took them to the beach

4 Did you say you were going to Paris tomorrow for a fortnight?
   (a) No, to Rome
   (b) No, for a week
   (c) No, the day after tomorrow

5 Is your son going by air to Paris?
   (a) No, my daughter is
   (b) No, he's going by train
   (c) No, he's going to Berlin

The final stress practice can be done using the picture below (sketched quickly with pin figures on the board perhaps).

Where's your mother?
She's downstairs.
(down, stairs – even stress)

Is your mother upstairs?
No, she's DOWNstairs
(down – extra stress)

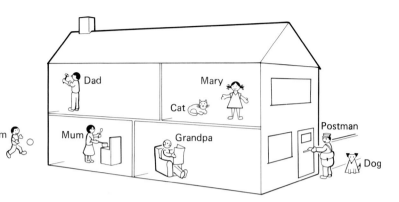

In an open question like 'Where's your mother?', the answer 'She's downstairs' will have even stress on *down* and *stairs.* If the answer to the question *corrects* something in the question, extra stress will be given to the correction.

Is your mother upstairs?   (even stress)
No. She's DOWNstairs   (down – extra stress)

Intonation

Remember that how you say something can sometimes – particularly with one word or a short phrase – be more important than what you say. Very often you will find pupils have done pronunciation practice but not practice in stress and intonation. Here are some useful intonation practices.

'One word' questions and 'or' questions
Say these examples making a clear difference between the different kinds of question.
1 Bread?   5 Soup or fruit juice?
2 Butter?   6 Fish or meat?
3 Salt and pepper?   7 Boiled potatoes or chips?
4 Mustard?   8 Beer or wine?
Now do these examples, but be careful, as the different kinds of questions are mixed together.
 9 A glass of wine?   12 Sugar?
10 Red, white or rose? 13 Soup or something else?
11 Black or white?   14 Soup?

'Question' word questions and 'Yes/No' questions
Questions which expect the answer Yes or No have a different pattern from those which begin with a question word. Practise with the following:
1 Are you having a holiday soon?
  When are you going?
2 Is it an expensive trip?
  How much will it cost?
3 Have you bought a new outfit?
  Where did you get it?
4 Are you going on your own?
  Who are you going with?
5 Are you going by air?
  Which airport do you go from?
6 Are you going to London?
  Where are you going?
7 Does it take long?
  How long does it take?
8 Will you be away for long?
  How long do you expect to be away?
9 Are you coming back before Whitsun?
  When are you coming back?
10 Is there a special reason for this trip?
  Why are you going?
11 Won't you let me into the secret?
  Why don't you let me into the secret?

Questions and surprise

A single word or a short phrase can be made into a question if your voice goes up at the end. It can also be said to show surprise (demonstrate clearly to pupils using, for example, *tomorrow*? and *tomorrow*!).

Say these words and phrases as questions:

1 Twelve?	6 Ten pounds?	11 Fifty?
2 Spain?	7 Six o'clock?	12 This evening?
3 By car?	8 Jill?	13 At Christmas?
4 Next week?	9 Your mother?	14 Three weeks?
5 A month?	10 Yesterday?	15 London?

Now practise in pairs using the following:

A: Tomorrow? (as a suggestion/question)
B: Tomorrow! (surprise at the suggestion)

Attitudes

You can show different attitudes by *how* you say a single word or phrase (or even by making the sound *mmmmm* in a certain way).

Can you show doubt, enthusiasm, and surprise by saying the following:

Yes	Thank you	I see	Oh
Of course	Certainly	Really	
mmmm			

Pupils can work in pairs with these dialogues:

Surprise
1 *A*: I met Prince Philip today
  B: Prince Philip!
2 *A*: I'm going to Africa next week
  B: Africa!

Doubt
1 *A*: I'm sure that was Prince Philip
  B: Prince Philip . . .
2 *A*: You've always wanted to go to Africa, haven't you?
  B: Africa . . .

Pupils can practise in pairs (using all three responses) with the following:

1 I haven't seen Bill for ages	9 I had a fight with him
2 Switzerland was a bit dull	10 We were at school together
3 She's just passed her driving test	11 They've got a lovely house
4 She's getting married	12 He's going to England
5 He's a famous actor	13 It wasn't a very good game
6 It's pretty expensive	14 I bought it in London
7 He's just bought a moped	15 I'm playing tennis on Saturday
8 He was really annoyed	16 I can't find my pen anywhere

Enthusiasm
1 *A*: Is there anyone you'd like to meet?
  B: Prince Philip!
2 *A*: Where shall we go next year?
  B: Africa!

Here are some more suggestions for those practices:

The Queen	China
The President	Leningrad
Margaret Thatcher	Moscow
Princess Margaret	Aberdeen
Jimmy Carter	Tipperary
Henry Kissinger	South America
Sophia Loren	Munich
John Lennon	Iceland
The Prime Minister	On Concorde
Robert Redford	Switzerland

Active listening

Whenever two people are having a real conversation they are both taking part all the time. Even if one does most of the talking, the other shows interest in different ways. He can, for example, look at his partner and smile, nod, say *mmmm, mmmm,* or *Oh yes I see.*

We also encourage the other person to speak using these patterns:

I've just been to Italy
Really?

I've just been to Italy
Italy?

I've just been to Italy
Have you?

This point can be practised further, and perhaps more naturally, by giving individual pupils a card containing information. They can then talk using the information while another pupil 'listens actively'. Here are some examples of the sort of information that can go on the card:

1 Skiing holiday you're thinking of going on — Austria — rather expensive — going alone — prefer to go with someone — need to buy new boots — doubtful.
2 Last month — the flu — two weeks off school — stay in bed — tired all the time — couldn't eat much — felt miserable — an old friend visited you — he'd been living in Africa.
3 New car you've just bought — sold your old Volvo — new one much faster — nice colour — quieter — warmer in the winter.
4 New boss in your office — very strict — works hard — married — no family — shouted at his secretary — not very popular.
5 Book you've just read — best detective story — exciting — only cost a few pence — better than watching TV.
6 Film you saw last week — cost £2 for a seat — it was worth it — about a man who murders his wife — frightening in places — think you'll go again.

3.4   Simple oral drills

Grammar practice probably conjures up in your own mind written work and endless fill-in exercises from your school days. In contrast to that drudgery the oral drill is a much more entertaining (and probably more efficient) way of practising simple grammar points in a controlled way. The practice may be done either T – C (you, the teacher T, give a prompt and the whole class chorus the response), or T – P (individual pupils respond in turn).

Particularly if you have less able classes or younger classes where 'having a conversation' is impossible, the drill which involves everybody and means many people speak a lot of correct English, is very worthwhile.

1   A SIMPLE FLUENCY PRACTICE
(See also articulation practices, pp. 23–6)

The idea of these drills is self-explanatory — fluency. Take a simple grammar point and make the class change a sentence quickly by inserting a new element given by the teacher. From a practical point of view the drills are not as simple as they look. The first time you try it with pupils, it's easiest to write the first few steps on the blackboard to show them what they are expected to do. Having done that, you can go on to use the idea again and again, since the class knows what is expected of it.

3rd person -s: He likes tea
T: Say after me: I like coffee
C: I like coffee
T: We
C: We like coffee
T: Tea
C: We like tea
T: He
C: He likes tea
T: Hate
C: He hates tea
T: My mother
C: My mother hates tea
T: My parents
C: My parents hate tea
T: My sister
and so on

much/many
T: Say after me: I haven't got much time
C: I haven't got much time
T: Money
C: I haven't got much money
T: Books
C: I haven't got many books
T: Information
C: I haven't got much information
and so on

2   A TRANSFORMATION DRILL

So . . . I
Neither . . . I
T: I like cheese
C: So do I
T: I can swim
C: So can I
T: I'm going swimming
C: So am I

T: I can't play tennis
C: Neither can I
T: I don't know Mary very well
C: Neither do I

He's a tall man
Yes, he's the tallest man I know
T: He's a rich man
C: Yes, he's the richest man I know
T: She's a poor woman
C: Yes, she's the poorest woman I know
T: He's a short man
C: Yes, he's the shortest man I know

This is another practice which can be done with the minimum amount of material. The teacher needs a slip of paper or a card with his prompts, and a blackboard to write up the first few examples to give the class the pattern. The practice depends on the speed with which you do it. The whole idea is that pupils should be forced to respond automatically, ie they improve their fluency, and ability to manipulate basic English structures.

Notice how little the teacher says in these drills. He should just be giving the prompts and no more. If the drill breaks down or the pupils get lost, no explanation is needed; just go back one step to an example they did correctly. In all of these drills it's important that the teacher has worked out BEFORE the lesson the prompts he's going to use − it's best to have made a list of them on, for example, a library card so that you can keep the prompts before you while doing the drill. If you try to do them without preparing all the examples before the class you'll find yourself producing examples like this:

T: He's a black man
C: Yes, he's the blackest man I know

or this

T: She's an attractive woman
C: Yes, she's the attractivest woman I know

These drills depend for their effectiveness on the speed at which they are done. There simply won't be time for you to think up the examples in class. Make sure you're prepared!

3 POINTS TO DRILL

Here are some common points which lend themselves to the kind of drilling we have just mentioned.

(1) I *live* at home He *lives* at home	3rd person -'s'
(2) I *play* tennis every Tuesday I'*m playing* tennis next Tuesday	Present simple for something happening regularly; continuous for something in the future
(3) How *much* money / *many* apples have you got?	*Many* used with countable nouns *Much* used with uncountables, ie nouns we do not see as units.
(4) I haven't got *much* time / *many* friends	
(5) I've got a *few* books / a *little* money	*A few* used with countables *A little* used with uncountables
(6) He's a *dangerous* driver He drives *dangerously*	Formation of (regular) adverbs by adding -ly to the adjective
He's a *good* player He plays *well*	Irregular adverbs

(7) I've been married *since* 1978
I've been married *for* three years

Since with points of time
For with periods

(8) I've *just* seen John
Oh, *have* you? I *saw* him yesterday

Difference between past simple (*saw*)
and present perfect (*have seen*)

(9) I've just been to America
Oh, *have* you?

Repetition of the auxiliary verb to show
interest

I leave tomorrow
Oh, *do* you?

Use of (do) when there is no auxiliary
verb

(10) He's *taller* than I am
He's *more intelligent* than me

Regular comparative adjectives and
those requiring *more*

(11) He's from *Italy*
Yes, he's *Italian*
Of course, he speaks *Italian*

Countries, adjectives, and languages

(12) They're married
They're married *aren't they*

Adding the tag to a statement

(13) *Have* you *got* a pen
Yes, I've *got* one

Use of *have got* not *have*, and use of
some in simple positive sentences

Have you *got* any money?
Yes, I've *got some*

(14) a television
— he's *going to* watch TV
a camera
— he's *going to* take some pictures

The *going to* future where there is
evidence now for the future action or
event

(15) It belongs to me
— It's *mine*
It belongs to John
— It's *John's*

Possessive adjectives: mine, yours, his,
hers, ours, theirs, Mary's, the
Smiths', etc.

(16) I can swim — So *can* I
I can't swim — Neither *can* I
I play tennis — So *do* I
I don't play tennis — Neither *do* I

Use of *so/neither* with the auxiliary
verb to agree

(17) She knows him
— *Does* she know him?
She went there
— *Did* she go there?

Making questions with (do)

(18) I like coffee
— I *don't* like coffee

Making negatives with (do)

(19) I go there a lot
— I *don't* go there *very much*
I thought it was lovely
— I *didn't* think it was *very nice*

Making negatives where other parts of
the sentences must change, especially
use of: *not very* + positive adjective

(20) Rain/get wet
— If it *rains* you'*ll get* wet
Come/be disappointed
— If you *come* you'*ll be* disappointed

Formation of simple conditionals (likely)

(21) Drive when you're drunk   Difference between *mustn't* and *don't*
   – You *mustn't* drive when you're drunk   *have to*
  Give people lifts
   – You *don't have to* give people lifts

(22) Lovely house   *a* used with countable nouns and never
   – What *a* lovely house   with plurals or uncountables
  Lovely cottages
   – *What* lovely cottages
  Nice weather
   – *What* nice weather

(23) Tuesday – *on* Tuesday   Prepositions
  Summer – *in* summer
  Christmas – *at* Christmas

In a few cases where the teacher's prompt is a question and two different answers would be produced according to whether the pupil replies positively or negatively the teacher can of course dictate which he wants by, for example, nodding or shaking his head as he finishes his own question.

3.5   Language games

Games have a place in any classroom, firstly from the point of view of motivation. All learning involves some rather mundane work. Clearly, if the teacher can build material such as irregular verbs into a game, he stands a greater chance of motivating pupils, especially in younger classes. Secondly, many games generate language ideal for the *language* classroom, providing the teacher has a clear idea of what language he expects the pupils to have to use in order to play the game.

In general, language games should be used for revision practice and should only take up a small part of the lesson. They provide variety in the middle of a lesson or in the last five or ten minutes. However, there is nothing against basing the whole lesson on a more complex game provided that it is then clear to the pupils that the game is being used to TEACH them language. Below we have given some of the most common types of games with examples to help you make up your own.

1   ALPHABET GAMES

These games are aimed more at younger pupils. The basic idea is that the teacher sets a theme and the pupils then go round the class, each giving a word beginning with the next letter of the alphabet.

(a) Holidays
Teacher starts: *I'm going on holiday to Africa*
First pupil says: *And I'm going to Bulgaria*
Second pupil: *And I'm going to China*

This then goes round the class, each pupil repeating the sentence with a new country. It can also be done with capital cities, or names of English towns.

(b) The last letter game
Teacher starts by giving one word; for example, *dangerous*. Pupil 1 gives *silly*. Pupil 2, *yacht*, and so on, where the next pupil says any word that comes into his head, starting with the last letter of the previous word.

(c) Jobs
Teacher starts: *When I leave school I'm going to become an architect*

First pupil: *And I'm going to become a bus driver*
And so on round the class with jobs.

(d) Adjectives
Teacher starts: *On my way here I saw an awful accident*
Pupil 1: *And I saw a broken-down bus*
Pupil 2: *And I bought a cheap pair of shoes*
And so on, each pupil saying something that he did, saw, bought, etc. using an adjective beginning with the next letter.

2 QUESTIONING GAMES

These depend on one pupil having some information or pretending to be something and the rest of the class asking questions to find out what it is.

(a) What's my line?
A pupil volunteers to start. He thinks of a job and comes to the front of the class. Pupils then ask him questions to find out what his job is. This game generates questions in the present tense beginning with *do*. Before it starts, the teacher must tell the class how they are to ask the questions, ie round the class or by putting their hands up. Twenty-five pupils shouting questions at the same time is chaos. It's also a good idea with younger classes to suggest before the game starts some of the questions they might ask. For example:

Is your job usually done by a man/woman?
Do you wear a uniform of any kind?
Do you work indoors/outdoors?
Do you work alone?
Is your job a glamorous/dangerous one?
Do you use any tools?
Do you make things?
Do you need a university degree for your
  job?
Do you work in a factory/office/hospital
  etc. . . .?
Are you a . . .?

(b) Who am I?
This is a variation on the previous one, except that the pupil at the front is either a famous personality from the present or from history. It is best if the teacher decides on the character and slips a piece of paper to the pupil with the name written on it. (Remember, people who are dead generate *did* questions.)
Other variations: *I've just been given a present, what do you think it is? What do you think I'm going to do this weekend? Where am I going on holiday? What did I do last night?* This forces the pupils to use the *going-to* future in questions (for example, *Are you going to watch television?*).

(c) Twenty questions
The class ask one person questions about a mystery object (decided on by the teacher). They are given some information at the beginning (it's a place/thing etc. for younger classes, the more difficult radio format can be used for older pupils). They are then allowed twenty questions to find out what it is.

(d) The yes/no game
The teacher goes round the class in turn (perhaps use teams for younger children) asking rapid questions. The words Yes and No are not allowed in the answer. A pupil using one of those words must drop out. This of course forces pupils to use alternative manipulative or functional answers (*I do, I have, that's right, I'm afraid you're mistaken*). The winner is the pupil who lasts out without using Yes or No.

Hint: As questioner, repeat the answers as they are given to you, eg:

Q: What time did you get up this morning?
A: Seven o'clock.
Q: Seven o'clock?
A: Yes. (*A* has to drop out)

3 DESCRIBING GAMES

The principle here is that one pupil describes something to the others who endeavour to guess the object, place, etc. The game is probably best played in teams and points scored if the team cannot guess 'who' or 'what' after being given, say, six pieces of information.

(a) Nationalities
Give individual pupils a card on which is written a nationality (a Lapp, a Frenchman, a Scotsman, etc.). Each pupil has to talk a little about what he wears, thinks, eats, likes, and so on as if he were a person of that nationality.

(b) Where am I?
Give individual pupils cards on which are written the name of a place. A pupil has to talk about the place answering these questions:

What can you see?
What can you hear?
What are the people around you doing?

For elementary groups use simple places, eg the railway station, the cinema, etc. For more advanced groups try more difficult places, eg Madame Tussaud's, in a submarine, etc.

(c) What am I doing?
A pupil has to describe what he is doing. He scores one point for each statement he makes about it before the other team guesses what he's doing. He must describe it accurately and in the proper sequence.

With less able groups you may want to give them the actions on cards, eg making a cup of coffee, unlocking and opening a door, packing a suitcase, and so on.

4 TEAM GAMES

Many pupils, particularly younger ones, enjoy competing in teams against each other. Here are some suggestions:

(a) Hiding and Finding
This is basically a vocabulary and grammar practice game.

First, the teacher draws a house on the board and asks the pupils, 'I'm standing in the kitchen/hall/sitting room, what can I see?' The class supplies vocabulary items for furniture, etc.

Then the class is divided into teams. The teacher says, 'I bought my mother a Christmas present and I want to hide it somewhere so she can't find it. See if you can find out where I've hidden it. Each team can ask me a question in turn but I can only say Yes or No and the team that guesses where the present is gets a point.'

Pupils may need some help with the questions which should lead towards the correct answer, eg:

Is it upstairs/downstairs? Is it in the sitting room/kitchen/big bedroom? It is behind/under/in/on etc, something (to establish which preposition is appropriate). Is it under the bed/bookcase/etc?

Obviously it's also possible to let a pupil 'hide' something. Different grammatical forms are possible for the question:

Did you hide it . . .?
Have you hidden it . . .?
Will you put it . . .?
Are you going to put it . . .?

The game can also be extended to 'When I was in London I lost my pen' and similar variations.

(b) Associations
The old game where someone starts with a word and the next person says the first word that comes into their head. If challenged on a word a player must be able to explain the association; for example aeroplane, airport, customs, passport, photograph etc.

(c) Suitcase game
Imagine you're going on holiday. What will you put in your suitcase? The game goes round the class, each person giving a different thing they will take with them. (It can be made more difficult by making it an alphabet game too, making all words begin with the same or consecutive letters).

(d) Building

The teacher or one of the class says any letter. The next player has to add another, and the third another and so on; but each additional letter must be one more to the correct spelling of a word. The object of the game is to keep going as long as possible without finishing a word. Any player who finishes a word loses a life; anyone losing three lives is out of the game. All letters added must be leading to a word; if one player adds a letter which another player thinks is not building up to a word, then that player may be challenged to say what word he was thinking of. If he cannot answer he loses a life; if he gives a correct word then the challenger loses a life.

(e) Vocabulary Games

The class is divided into teams. The teacher gives an area of vocabulary, eg adjectives to describe people; each team then collects words and the group with the most examples after, say, five minutes wins. A variation is to let one member of the team write the words on the blackboard: words that are spelt wrongly lose points.

Possible areas of vocabulary could be food (for breakfast/lunch), the home, furniture, jobs, buildings, kinds of tree, kinds of flowers, sports, transport, names of countries etc.

3.6   Using pictures in class

As with all material, if you are clear why you are using it, it will usually be a success. The success of pictures depends largely on practical considerations. Make sure your pictures are large enough and you have enough of them. A single picture will usually work in a group of up to 8, but in larger groups divide the class and use several pictures. Even in small classes it is advisable to stick pictures on to a piece of firm card.

Clearly the best pictures can be used for several different purposes with the same or different classes. At lower levels they are used mostly for naming things, describing events or telling a story. At higher levels pictures should be ambiguous, permitting different interpretations to allow the class to speculate or discuss.

If you think you are going to have lower level classes, or are keen to use pictures and want more specific guidance we suggest you refer to *The Magazine Picture Library* by Janet McAlpin (Allen and Unwin, 1980) which discusses the choice and use of pictures in detail. (There is also a ready-made source of picture material in a book called *What do you think?* by D. Byrne and A. Wright (Longman, 1974).

The drawings, pictures and related questions below are to serve only as examples. The Colour Supplements provide an obvious source of alternatives but it is important to remember that the main criterion for selection is the *language* the picture will generate.

NOTES ON PICTURES

A

See p. 60.

B
(i) Describe these people's appearance.
(ii) What are they like? Describe their personality.
(iii) What do you think they do for a living?
(iv) What nationality are they? How did you decide?
(v) Given the choice, who would you like to be?

C
(i) What do these stand for? Can you think of a clearer sign for the same thing? (*Answers:* 1. Waiting room. 2. Escalator. 3. Car hire. 4. Fountain. 5. Winter sports. 6. Picnic place. 7. Dentist. 8. Theatre.)

D
(i) What is happening?
(ii) Describe what they are wearing.
(iii) What are the two families like?
(iv) Where do the two families live?
(v) What are their jobs?
(vi) Will the couple be happy?
(vii) Does a wedding look like this in your country?

A

B

C

 1

2

3

4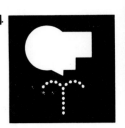

5

6

7

8

D

E

(i) What is the man doing? Why?

(ii) Where is he going?

(iii) Pair work. One pupil saw this happening. He is now at home talking to his wife. She says, *Anything special happen today, dear?*

F

(i) Where do you think this is? When was the picture taken?

(ii) How will it have changed if you see it now?

(iii) What did people use to do/wear/think in those days?

G

(i) Where do you think this is?

(ii) How do you know?

(iii) How do you know it is not your country?

(iv) Would you like to live in this city?

G

H

(i) What are these people doing?

(ii) Last night someone was mending a fuse and all the lights went out. What were they doing when the lights went out?

(iii) Last night someone was murdered in the house. The lights went out mysteriously at 9 o'clock. A policeman has come to investigate. (One pupil interviews others in groups). What did the policeman tell his wife that night when he went home and she asked *Did anything exciting happen today?* Work in pairs and continue the conversation.

H

3.7   Discussion topics

The conversation lesson built round a topic-based discussion is one of the most difficult lessons to make work. This is particularly true with younger or less able pupils. However, you may either be asked to do this or want to try for yourself.

(i)   You must have a specific objective in mind. It's no good going in with the idea of talking about smoking. There are probably at least three or four different lessons there – smoking and health, smoking and advertising, and smoking in public places. Of course this does not mean you over-restrict pupils but the more specific you are able to keep the discussion, the greater the language practice they are getting, and the more topics you will have at your disposal for later in the year.

(ii)   If you are able to take into the room something concrete you will usually find it easier to start a discussion in a natural way.

LIST OF TOPICS FOR DISCUSSION

Comparison with the host country
Although not a particular topic, making the pupils talk about various aspects of their own country is one of the most useful themes you can use in your discussion lessons. There is little point in your telling classes about Britain for the sake of it, but there is every point in doing so in order to stimulate the pupils to talk in a similar way about their own country. You should try and use this tactic wherever possible in the following suggested topics. It is particularly applicable to topics such as food, education, social customs and behaviour, language and all aspects of society.

Host town/host country
What are the main attractions/industries of your town? Where would you take a visitor/definitely not take a visitor?

What could be done to improve your town? Make a list of its facilities and where it is deficient.

Draw an outline map of the country on the board. Tell the class that it is to be buried so that hundreds of years from now people will be able to dig it up and find out what their country was like. Ask different groups to mark on it three places with beautiful scenery/important industries/suitable for holidays/famous in history/famous for good food/centres for sport/old customs etc.

You have an American cousin coming to visit you for two weeks. You would like to show him the country. Plan a two-week trip round your country.

What makes you proud to be (French etc.)? Is there anything in your country you're ashamed of? What are the main/best/worst characteristics of your countrymen?

Florence is a very industrialised city isn't it? Remember that to make a wrong statement about the host country will very often stimulate much more discussion than a question. Pupils love to correct their misinformed teachers.

Free time activities
(a) Hobbies
What hobbies do you have? How long do you spend on them? How often? Do they cost a lot? Why would you recommend your hobbies to other people?

Discuss *'Hobbies should be taught in school otherwise people won't know what to do with them with their free time,'* or
   'Someone who has no hobbies does not know what life is about.'

(b) Sport
What sports do you play?
   Do you prefer team games or individual games?
   Persuade someone else in the class they should play the sports that you play.
   'People shouldn't worry about winning. It's enough just to take part.'
   Do you think that sports competitions between countries help international understanding?
   Did you watch the last Olympic Games? Were they political?

'A huge political hoax or the greatest aid to world peace.'

These are two common views of the Olympics. What do you think? Do your parents agree?

At the moment, sport is paid for by the people who watch it, whereas the arts are paid for very largely by state subsidies. Is this fair?

'It's wrong to compete against countries like South Africa.'
'Nonsense, the more contact we have with them the more likely we are to change them.'

'Boxing – it's not a sport, it's cruel.'
'Gambling – sport's about doing things for fun, not making money.'
'I hate sport on television – there's no atmosphere.'
'It must be awful to be a professional sportsman, *having* to win. Sport should be for fun.'

(c) The arts
Classical music, the opera, ballet, the theatre etc.; have you ever been to any of these? Where? When? What did you see/hear?

Do you know anyone who *never* goes to any of these? What facilities are there in your town for them?

'Opera is a minority interest so why should the majority pay anything for it.' What do you think? People who live in country areas have got to pay income tax so that people in the big cities can go to ballet. Is this fair?

Your local library – can you borrow books? Records? Listen to music at the library? What other facilities has it got?

'The theatre is much more exciting than the cinema or television!'

Would you like to be an actor? Why/why not?

The family
How many brothers and sisters have you got? What are they called? What do they do?

What about your cousins/uncles/aunts/grandparents? Draw a family tree for your family and say a bit about everybody.

Age
What's your first memory?

Can you remember your first day at school? Why do you remember that in particular?

Do you believe there is a *generation gap*?

Work in groups and discuss what has changed most since your parents/grandparents were your age.

What kind of things do you disagree most about with older people? Whose fault is it?

Do you agree or disagree about the following:
1 Girls should not get married before they're 21.
2 I'd rather take my holidays with my parents.
3 All families should spend two hours together at home every evening.
4 Parents ought to be stricter with their children.
5 If I had a problem I'd always go to my parents rather than my friends.
6 Parents should let their children buy their own clothes.

What do you think is the ideal age to get married? Should people always marry people of their own age?

'20 year old girl marries 70 year old millionaire.' What do you think of that?

What do you think is the ideal age?
(Notice here that, rather than an abstract discussion, it is much better to use half-a-dozen sentences with the 'do you agree with these or not' technique. It is easy to make up a further set of your own.)

Clothes
Make a list of men's clothes/women's clothes (Include also types of material).

Do you buy your own clothes?

How do you choose your clothes – to last, or to be in fashion?

'Fashion is just a way of wasting money.' Do you agree?

(This is much more difficult than most people think. With lower levels it usually only consists of making a list of vocabulary. Most people find it difficult to have a discussion about clothes.)

Boys-v-Girls

Is your school mixed? Do you think it should/should not be?

'Girls should be allowed to play football and boys should be allowed to learn cooking.' What do you think?

Are there any jobs that only men or women should do? What are they, and why do you think that?

If your father went to the doctor and found she was a woman what would he think?

'The women's libbers have confused equality with similarity.' What do you think this means and do you agree?

'Modern girls expect too much – the same opportunities and boys to take them out, pay for them, and so on.'

'Boys/men have more fun in life than girls/women.'

'Men and women really are different – why pretend they are the same?'

Food

What have you had to eat today? What do you normally have for breakfast/lunch/dinner?

What's your favourite food? Which do you hate most?

What food is your country famous for? What about the region where you live?

Are there many restaurants in your town? Are there any foreign ones? Do you ever eat out? Where? Why? Design your ideal meal. What would you eat? Who would you invite?

If you're in a hurry, what do you normally make yourself to eat? Are we losing our standards of eating because of convenience foods? What food would you like to see banned?

Relationships

How many brothers and sisters have you? Are they your friends? Do you fight much? What about?

What sort of people are your friends? Are they all of the same age? Are you interested in the same things? Why are they your friends?

Do you ever read the problem page in magazines? Have you ever written to one? What kind of people write to them? What are 'typical problems'?

Newspapers/magazines/comics

What was the last newspaper/magazine/comic that you bought? Do you buy it regularly? Why? Describe it. Does your town have a local newspaper? What's it like? What kind of things does it report? What kind of newspapers and magazines can you buy from your local newsagent?

What did today's papers say? What are the most important newspapers in your country? When and where are they published? Which do your parents read? Why?

A lot of things that get into the newspapers are not really news. What kind of thing do you think is important to read about in the newspapers? What kind of thing would you like to see disappear from newspapers?

Are all the newspapers in your country objective? Talk about the different ones and say what their political standpoint is.

'There won't be any newspapers in 20 years time – just a little electronic machine in your sitting room.' Do you agree?

Holidays

Where did you go on your last holiday? What did you do? Who went with you? What was it like? Will you go back there?

What's important about a good holiday? Put the following in order of importance: sunshine, few people, good food, beautiful scenery, theatres, opera, swimming, museums, good shops, discos, etc.

Work in groups of four and plan your dream holiday.

Bicycles, mopeds and cars

Do you have a bike/moped/car? Who bought it? Do you really need it?

'People who drive mopeds should be forced to take a driving test and wear a crash helmet all the time.' What do you think? Make a list of all the parts of your bike/moped in English.

Have you done anything special to your bike/moped? How would someone know it was yours?

'No one needs a car, but a lot of people need a status symbol.' This is a common view of why people own a car. Do you/your parents own a car? What do you/they need it for? (*The Driving Instructor* by Bob Newhart is an entertaining introduction to this topic, if you can get a recording of it.)

People should take a driving test every 5 years.

Old people shouldn't be allowed to drive – after all, young people aren't allowed to.

If you could own any car you wanted, which would you have? Why?

Traditions and festivals

Every country celebrates Christmas in its own special way. What do you do at Christmas? Do your family all come together? When do you give presents? What do you eat?

At what other times of the year do you do something special? Do you dress up in any way? Does your country have a national costume? When do people wear it? Do you have one? What's it like?

When was the last time you sent a card? Do you just send them on people's birthdays?

Have you ever been to a wedding? What was it like? How were people dressed? What did they do?

(Obviously you should exploit any local custom/dress, etc. here.)

Television and radio

Do you have a television and radio at home? Is the television black and white or colour? How often do you listen or watch every day? Do you know anyone who does not have television? Why don't they?

Describe a typical evening on television in your country? What sort of programme do you particularly like?

Plan an evening's television with all your favourite programmes (see p. 57.) If your television was taken away tomorrow what would you do in the evenings instead?

'Television has not only destroyed the art of conversation but is also the single biggest factor in teenage violence.' What do you think?

Is television basically a good or bad thing?

'People are better informed because of TV.'

'TV is dangerous – you don't know what is real and what is fantasy.'

Travelling around Europe

What other European countries have you visited? How did you travel? Where did you stay?

Have you ever Inter-railed? Where did you go? What did you do? Did you spend all your time travelling? Or did you see any of the country?

Have you ever had a holiday job in another country? What did you do? What was it like?

Plan a month travelling round Europe (with a free ticket won in a competition).

What are the main differences between the French/Spanish/Germans/Italians/British?

Money

Do your parents give you pocket money: if so, how much, or do you have a little job of your own?

People are always trying to win money, but what would you do if you won a lot?

What would you do if you won a) £10, b) £1,000, c) £20,000, d) £1,000,000?

What would your parents do in the same situations? Would winning a lot of money change you as a person?

Schools

Have you always been at this school? If not, what were your other schools like?

Describe a typical day at school. What do you most like/most dislike about school?

Make up your ideal weekly timetable.

Some British schools still use corporal punishment. What do you think of this? Does your school have it? Do you think your school should have it?

When do children start school in your country? Is this too early/late?

When can you leave school? Do you think this should be changed?

What do you most want to see changed in your education system?

Is it easy to carry on studying when you leave school? Do you have to pay for further education, or do you get a grant?

'Education should be theoretical. Practical education is not real education.' What do you think?

'We should learn more/less about other countries/practical things like buying a flat/how to use our free time/other people and how they think . . .'

'It's a waste of time reading Shakespeare/Molière/Goethe in the 1980s.' Do you agree?

Should school be as much like 'the outside world' as possible or not? Why?

'Schools encourage competition — that's a bad thing. We should learn to work together in school.'

Jobs

Think of as many jobs as you can.

Which of these would you think of doing yourself?

What's your father's/mother's/brother's/sister's job?

Are there any jobs you would not do?

(This topic is very often much less successful than you expect. Most jobs in fact do not have specific names. The best lessons are those based on a specific activity to do with jobs. You will find the following pages provide concrete material for a good discussion. For example, *What's My Line*, p. 35, *the Balloon Debate*, p. 59, *What is a Good Job*, p. 52.)

People

(a) Appearance

Prepare a description of yourself, what you look like.

Describe other people in the class. Describe your teacher.

Choose somebody not in your class — a friend or a relative, or a famous person — and describe what they look like.

(b) Personality

Collect adjectives to describe people's characters and talk about some people that you know. What about yourself? What kind of person do you like/dislike?

Choose a famous person (that the pupils will have heard of) and describe his/her personality.

Have you ever filled in a personality questionnaire, for example a computer dating form? What do you think of them? (There's one on p. 63.)

(c) National characteristics

Everybody has an idea of a typical Frenchman/German/Italian/Spaniard. Can you describe all those nationalities? Is what people say about your country true?

Are you a typical Frenchman, etc.? Why/why not? What do people in your country think of the British? Do they think the English, the Irish, the Welsh and the Scots are all the same? The English think the Scots are mean, the Irish are a bit stupid and the Welsh sing well. Can you say similar things about the regions in your country?

'Of course you can't generalise about people.' What do you think?

Houses

Do you have a room of your own? Plan your ideal room. What kind of house/flat do you live in? How many rooms has it? Describe them. Plan your ideal house. Where is it? Town/country? How many rooms has it?

(For groupwork on houses see the estate agent problem on p. 60.)

Music

What kind of music do you like?

Do you play an instrument?

What kind of music do you not like?

'In a hundred years' time, people will have forgotten all the pop groups of the 70s and 80s except the Beatles.' Do you agree?

Why do people still listen to composers like Mozart, Verdi and Beethoven?

'I can't stand pop music — it's just a noise.' Is it?

Britain

Have you ever been to Britain?

What do you know about London?

(Underground map, brochures.)

Do you have a picture of the British as bowler-hatted, conservative with walking sticks? What are they really like? What about the (French)?

(Remember, the idea of a topic like this is NOT for the teacher to inform the foreigner about Britain. It is to present some ideas about Britain, or get the pupils talking about Britain in order that they can talk about their own experiences either in Britain or in their own country.)

The cinema

When was the last time you were at the cinema? What did you see? What kind of films do you like/dislike?

How many different kinds of film do you know?

Modern inventions

Make a list of things you use at home which didn't exist a hundred years ago.

Which four do you think you could easily do without and which four would you fight to keep?

Can you think of anything you would like to see invented? Something to make your life easier which does not exist at present.

What about all the people who have been thrown out of work by new inventions. What should we be doing with them?

Superstitions

Are you superstitious?

Are black cats walking under ladders special for you?

Make a list of things that are lucky/unlucky in your country. What about horoscopes? Do you read these/believe in them/are there any local superstitions/haunted houses/ghosts?

Why do you think people are superstitious?

Do you believe in UFOs? Have you seen any little green men/monsters (Loch Ness Monster/Abominable Snowman)?

The individual

The pupil's likes and dislikes: colours, clothes, records, books, sports, games, films, etc.

Pet hates: What really makes you mad? What punishment would you inflict on people who do things that you hate? Do you like/hate to be different from other people? Do you show your individuality? 'The worst thing you can say about anybody is that he's a conformist.' Do you agree?

Speech

Do you have an accent in your own language? What is different about your accent? Do you use any words which are not found throughout the whole country?

How many different languages are spoken in your country?

'Esperanto – a stupid idea, everyone should learn English.' What do you think?

Humour

Most English jokes make fun of some minority or other – for example, the Irish. Do you make fun of minorities in your jokes? If so, which ones? Do you tell jokes about people from other countries?

What sort of jokes do you find most funny/not funny at all?

Take along several British cartoons – are they funny or not? Why?

The following topics are most suitable for older classes. Do not attempt them with pupils younger than 16.

Crime

What would happen to someone in your country who had (a) stolen a shirt from a local supermarket, (b) murdered his wife, (c) not paid his television licence, (d) been caught driving while drunk, (e) broken into a house and stolen jewellery, (f) hit one of his children so hard that he'd broken the child's arm.

What do you think SHOULD happen to people who do those things?

The death penalty – does your country have it? Should it? For what crimes?

The environment

What industries are there near where you live? Is there any pollution from them?

Technology – science has moved forward more than ever in the past hundred years and has affected the environment greatly. Make a list of inventions/developments this century. Decide which have been harmful and which have been beneficial.

Argue for and against the following: *(a)* no cars in the cities, *(b)* jumbo jets, *(c)* disposable bottles, *(d)* plastic knives and forks.

Factories that pollute rivers/oil tankers that pollute the sea – which is worst? What should be done about them?

History

How long has your country been 'a country'? What is the first important date in its history?

Give six important dates in your country's history and say why they're important.

Why are the following dates important for the world: 570, 1564, 1812, 1492, 1789, 1930?

Every year, people remember the men and women who died in the two world wars. Do you think they will go on remembering? For how long?

Politics

'Politics has no place in school.' Do you agree?

What are the main issues in your country's politics at the moment? What are the main political parties in your country? Can you give a short description of their point of view? Have you ever protested against anything/been on a demonstration?

Military service

Is there conscription in your country? Who has to go? For how long? What happens if you refuse to go? Do you know anyone who has refused? 'People who refuse to do their military service are traitors to their country.' What do you think?

'If you're going to have military service then both boys and girls should have to do it. Why discriminate against boys?' What do you think? If there was another war, would you fight?

Fame

Pictures of famous people: who are they and why are they famous? Who are the ten most famous people in your country today and why? How many of them will be remembered in a hundred years' time?

Name six famous people from history who will always be remembered? Name six famous women from history.

Play the *Who am I?* game with famous people from the past.

Is fame the same as success?

Drinking

Have you ever drunk any alcohol? What was it and where?

Have your parents ever given you any alcohol to drink?

'Parents should teach their children how to drink at home.' When is the right time to start to teach children to drink?

America

Comparison of English and American words.

'America – the only true democracy in western Europe, or the most corrupt country in the world.' What do you think?

The Third World

Helping developing countries: have you ever given any money to help people in the Third World? Do you know what happens to your money?

'The rich countries aren't interested in the poor ones. They buy off their consciences every year with massive amounts of aid but it still isn't enough.' What should the rich countries of the world be doing?

Progress

The space race – has it been worth it? What spin-offs have there been?

The price of progress – televisions, jumbo jets, big cars, better hospitals, people living longer, plastic everything, washing machines, etc. – has it all been worth it? What have we lost?

Social behaviour

What do you do in the following social situations?

Introducing people who don't know each other/visiting someone for the evening/arriving at and leaving someone's house/giving someone a present/congratulating someone.

What can you say to someone you don't know in a railway compartment? What kind of things can you talk about/not talk about?

Advertising

Have you ever bought something because you saw it advertised?

Cigarette and alcohol advertising – do you think they should be banned?

Good adverts/bad adverts – have you a favourite advert? Are there any adverts that you do not like? How do adverts work? Do they affect you?

Minorities

Minority groups in your country: are there any and what are they fighting for?

Are you a member of any?

Immigrants – where do they come from? Why have they come to your country? Do you/they get a fair deal? (Remember that some of your class may be immigrants.)

Some types of discussion lesson

Before we look at concrete material it may be helpful to consider different sorts of discussion lesson.

Comparisons between England and the host country

This is an obvious theme which tends to run through all classes. There are concrete questions below for you to ask about the host country, but remember one of the easiest and best ways of stimulating pupils to react is to present them with information about their own country which is inaccurate or prejudiced.

Putting in order

You present a concrete list of items which students have to place in order of importance, value or whatever. These have the advantage of providing the concrete material for the discussions, and by choosing a suitable range of items you can make the discussions wider than

would be the case if you relied only on pupils' personal contributions.

A particular kind of problem which is often very popular and successful is the 'cornflake packet problem'. These are the sort of materials which are often the basis for competitions run by popular magazines or on the back of cereal packets. The basic idea is to 'put the following eight features of an ideal holiday in order of importance. If you think "sandy beaches" is most important number it 1 . . .'

The best – the worst – the ideal

Many obvious topics can be widened by asking pupils about them from three different points of view:

What's the best present you've ever been given?

What's the worst, most useless present you've been given?

If you could have anything at all you wanted for Christmas, what would it be?

Clearly, because you're asking about the best and worst, you tend to push the pupils into saying something more extreme, and therefore more interesting and discussable, than would otherwise be the case.

Role playing

There are basically two kinds. There are those where you put the student in a situation in which he may well find himself outside the classroom ('You're at the railway station and you want . . .'), which are obviously very much bound up with teaching dialogue and conversational work; and there is a more fantastic kind where students are given roles which they will never be likely to play ('You are the interviewer on a television programme. Your two guests are . . .')

Questionnaires

The sort of 'personality quiz' which is common in magazines can be a little childish, too risqué or too difficult linguistically. However, it could provide you with ideas for the kind you can make up yourself.

Debates

If you have older or capable pupils you may want to organise a debate. However, if you remember how much formal language and procedure is involved in this you will realise that it is a very difficult activity.

3.8 Practical materials for discussion topics

1 PUTTING IN ORDER

Win £1,000 for your holiday.

Look at the following list of attractions for your holiday. If you think the most important is 'beautiful scenery', write 1 beside it. Write 2 beside your next choice and so on. Then give one other feature that would specially appeal to *you*.

Sunshine . . .
Beautiful scenery . . .
Sandy beach . . .
Amusement arcade/bingo . . .
Good discos . . .
English spoken . . .
Interesting history . . .
Quiet, few people . . .
Good local food . . .

Win a new Kitchen for your Home

All you have to do is put the nine inventions listed below in the order you think they should go – mark the most useful 1, the next most useful 2 and so on . . . then add a new machine which you think would be useful in every home and which no one has invented yet.

A Fridge . . .
B Automatic washing machine . . .
C Deep freeze . . .
D Vacuum cleaner . . .
E Stereo hi-fi . . .
F Electric food mixer . . .
G Telephone . . .
H Dish washer . . .
I Tape Recorder . . .

My new machine is ....
....

The perfect partner

Everybody has a different idea of the ideal boyfriend or girlfriend. Put the following qualities in order of importance.

A Good looks . . .
B Patience . . .
C Plenty of money . . .
D Interests you both share . . .
E A sense of humour . . .
F Lets *you* decide things . . .
G Sexiness . . .
H Popular with your family . . .
I Popular with your other friends . . .

What makes a good job

When you're looking for a job, what things will make you think it is the job for you? Put these in order of importance.

A Well paid . . .
B Flexible hours . . .
C The chance to help other people . . .
D Lots of different things to do . . .
E Nobody tells you what to do . . .
F Long holidays . . .
G Lots of friendly people to work with . . .
H Power . . .

Help us to help you

We are planning a new magazine for all of you – boys and girls between 13 and 18. We want *you* to help us to make sure that you really enjoy our new magazine. Look at the features below and decide which is most important for you – number it 1, and so on, down to 9.

A A column answering your letters about personal problems . . .
B Good sports reports . . .
C News about the pop scene . . .
D Crosswords and puzzles . . .
E Letters from people the same age in other countries . . .
F A love story *every* week . . .
G Health and beauty tips . . .
H Technical reports about cars and scientific developments . . .
I Really attractive pin-up pictures . . .

It's a wonderful town

Think about the town you live in. Does it have all the things that you want. What sort of town would you really like to live in. Put the following features of towns in order.

A Lots of cinemas . . .
B A swimming pool . . .
C A good library . . .
D Late-night discos . . .
E Close to the countryside . . .
F Very little traffic . . .
G Nice architecture – fountains, parks and so on . . .
H A good local museum . . .

The ideal school

Look at the following statements about schools. Arrange them in order of importance – so that you will learn a lot and so that you will enjoy school. If there are any statements that you definitely do not agree with, write a new statement which gives your views about the same subject and put it in your list in the proper place.

A School should be about practical not theoretical things . . .
B Television should be used more to make school more interesting . . .
C Teachers should decide what is studied in school, not pupils . . .
D Everyone should study the same things . . .
E Parents should be allowed to come to classes . . .
F More time should be spent out of school – in the town doing things . . .
G Sport should be given a more important place at school . . .
H Everybody should have to study his own language, mathematics, the history of their country and English all the time they're at school . . .
I Schools should organise more social events for pupils – discos and so on . . .

Here is the news

Look at the following news items:

A Earthquake in Mexico, 200 people killed, 500 homeless
B Billie Jean King wins Wimbledon for the sixth time
C Socialists win French election

D Australian Prime Minister kidnapped
E Sydney Cutter murderer of six girls in six months arrested by police at airport
F *Sex in Cities* – called the most shocking film ever made – to be shown in London cinemas
G The Queen's flu is still not better

1 Which order do you think they *would* come in an English newspaper?
2 Is this the *right* order?

An important job

Which of the following jobs is the most important in your opinion? Put them in order:

Doctor
Policeman
Reporter
Soldier
Secretary
Farmworker
Politician
Dentist
Teacher
Pop singer
Miner
Minister

1 Which of them do you think earns most in your country nowadays?
2 Which of them do you think *should* earn most? Why?
3 Which of them would *you* like to do? Which *wouldn't* you like to do? Why?

A lovely evening

Here are six ways to spend an evening. Mark the one you would most like to do 1, and so on down to 6. Try also to give one way you would rather spend the evening than any of these. Can you also give one way you would really hate to spend the evening.

A Watching television . . .
B Playing tennis . . .
C Reading a novel . . .
D Having a serious discussion with your family . . .
E Working in the garden . . .
F Listening to records of Beethoven . . .

2 DO YOU AGREE?

Look at the following statements. Mark each one in the following way:

If you agree write 1.
If you disagree write 2.
If you are not sure about it write 3.

School

1 Teachers should keep pupils quiet in school.
2 Teachers talk too much.

3   Wearing uniforms is silly.
4   If a teacher doesn't know the answer, he should say 'I don't know'.
5   Corporal punishment can sometimes be a good idea.
6   The best age to start school is seven.
7   Teachers should teach their subject and not worry about what you're wearing, what you're doing and things like that.
8   Boys and girls should be treated exactly the same at school.
9   School at the moment is too easy.
10 School starts too early in the morning.

Men and women
1   Men are usually stronger than women.
2   Women are usually more sympathetic than men.
3   Women are usually better with children than men.
4   Women are usually better at running a home.
5   Men are better at making decisions than women.
6   Women are more careful than men.
7   Men lose their temper more easily than women do.
8   Women waste more time than men do.
9   Women work harder than men.
10 Men should treat women as equals, and women should treat men as equals but they don't.

In the next section, the figures on the right tell you what percentage of English boys and girls agreed with the statements in a recent survey.

The family

		Boys	Girls
1	Most parents ought to be stricter with their children.	54	47
2	Summer holidays without parents are more enjoyable.	63	65
3	Most teenagers are bored with their jobs.	36	30
4	It's best to have a good time before you get married because after that life's pretty dreary.	28	27
5	I learn more from my friends of my own age than I learn from my parents.	58	53
6	Today's teenagers are very different from teenagers in the past.	52	58
7	Teenage boys spend too much time thinking about their clothes and hair.	38	34
8	I'd rather go to my parents for advice than to my friends.	55	53
9	Teenagers should be able to go out in the evening without having to tell their parents where they're going.	55	40
10	Most adults say one thing but do another.	41	44

3 NATIONAL CHARACTERISTICS

Britain, land of tradition say the travel posters, but do these traditions really exist outside the pages of the tourist brochures? Ask ten people in a London street what they do, eat or wear at special times of the year and you'll probably get ten different answers.

Try this experiment yourselves. Here are some traditional beliefs about British people. Find out how 'typical' your English teacher is. Ask if he/she:

A Eats bacon and eggs for breakfast
B never drinks coffee, only tea
C has anyone in the family who wears a bowler hat
D lives in a thatched cottage
E went to a public school
F sings 'My Bonnie lies over the ocean' in the pub on Saturdays

Some students at an international centre in England were recently asked what they thought about the best and worst characteristics of their own countries. Here are some of their answers — do you agree with them?

A *Helmut (German)*
We're a very efficient people, we organise things well. I don't think we have a negative characteristic; people call us nationalistic but I'd say we were just proud of Germany.

B *Nadine (French)*
We have the best food in the world and the most beautiful language in the world. suppose we've made the biggest contribution to the history of Europe. I can't think of anything negative to say about my country, I think France is marvellous.

C *Mario (Italian)*
Oh, the Italians are alive. We enjoy life and doing things. In some ways we're a bit too light-hearted, but I think that's a good thing. Live for today — tomorrow's a long way away.

D *Torsten (Swedish)*
We are fair, we always try to see all sides of a problem and to consider everybody. suppose this makes us a bit slow to offer an opinion sometimes, we're *too* careful.

E *Maria (Spanish)*
I think we're rather a cruel people — think of bullfighting for example, which I hate. But we're very warm and generous. We try to help people — but we're not very nice to animals.

Are you a 'typical' member of your own country? Why/why not? What about your father/mother?

Give three adjectives *you* associate with:

Germans
Italians
Frenchmen
Swedes
Spaniards
Englishmen

4 GROUP DISCUSSIONS

The following materials are all suitable for use in a class which has been divided into small groups with a secretary and chairman appointed. Discussions may take place in English or their native language, but the reports and subsequent discussion should, of course, be in English. *You* should decide who goes in which group. Decide the distribution of stronger and weaker pupils to ensure as much activity as you can.

Group work 1
Plan what clothes the following will need to pack:

A A businessman flying to a three-day conference in Vienna in February.

B A couple going on their honeymoon for three weeks in June in the Mediterranean.
C A student travelling with an Inter-rail pass with a rucksack for a month.
D An 18-year-old girl going to stay for a weekend with friends in the country.
E A young couple going for a ski-ing holiday.

Group work 2
The Pyramids
Grand Canyon
Stonehenge
The Grand Canal
St Peter's Square
Notre Dame
  If you had to name three places in the world that you would like to see, which would you choose?
  Are they man-made or natural places?
  Which wins first prize? Why?
  Plan a trip around the world. Discuss:
  How will you travel from place to place? Where would you go? What do you hope to do and see?
  If you could take one (famous) person with you, who would you take? Why?

Group work 3
You are going to be cast away on a desert island with a record player and six records (fortunately the island has electricity!). There will only be the three of you on the island, and you have to agree on the six records you are going to take.

Group work 4
Look at the 'typical' evening's television programmes given below. Some of the programmes will appeal to you, but some of them won't. Work in groups to plan an evening's viewing (from 6 o'clock until the end of the day) so that there is something for everybody.

	BBC		ITV
5.50	News	5.45	News and Weather
6.00	London This Week − local news programme	6.00	Tom and Jerry Show
		6.20	Double Your Money
6.30	Ask the Family − a quiz for everyone	6.50	University Challenge
		7.20	Department S
7.00	The Virginian − Western film	8.15	Thursday Night Theatre − 'The Little Man'
8.15	Black and White Minstrel Show − light entertainment		
		10.00	News at Ten
9.00	News	10.30	The Saint
9.25	Ingrid Haebler plays Mozart	11.30	Late Night Movie − 'Frankenstein'
10.10	Invasion of Europe, 1940 − documentary: a report based on old news film		
11.00	The Brothers − serial		
11.30	Weather Forecast		

Group work 5
It's the year 2000. Everyone has their personal wrist computer for getting news and information, and your national government has decided that of radio, television, and newspapers only one can survive − not just for information but as a form of entertainment. Work in three groups, one each to defend radio, television and papers. Work out:

1 Why your medium is important.

2 What sort of service it can give to people (which they can't get from their wrist computers).

3 Why your service is better or more useful than the others.

Group work 6
Look at the following list of jobs. Say whether you think it would be best done by a) a man b) a woman or c) it doesn't matter. Give reasons why.

1 Babysitter
2 Doctor
3 Secretary
4 Newsreader on TV
5 Prime Minister
6 Teacher

Group work 7
What would your parents do in the following circumstances:

A You came home at 11 o'clock (11 pm).
B You came home at 1 o'clock (1 am).
C You smoked in your bedroom.
D You were sent home from school for disturbing the classes.
E You were caught stealing an LP in a local record shop.
F You wanted to have a party with 25 of your friends at home.
G You wanted to get married when you were only 17.
H You (or your sister) wanted to buy a moped.

Group work 8

Balloon Debate

A group of people are travelling in the balloon opposite, but it has a small hole in it and is falling. None of the people can swim. They decide one person must be thrown out, so that they can reach the (uninhabited) island.

Imagine you each have one of the jobs listed (by the teacher). Prepare a few reasons why you should not be thrown out. How will you help on the island? Why will the group need you? Who will they not need? After everyone has spoken, vote on who is going to be thrown out.

This game can also be played with more advanced classes by putting famous people in the balloon rather than jobs, eg Molière, Goethe, Wagner, Napoleon, Josephine.

Group work 9

Everyone gets annoyed sometimes – often for things that aren't very important. English people, for example, get annoyed if people don't queue. (Remember that if you go to England.) Here are the opinions of four people who say what really irritates them about other people – and how they think the people should be punished. What about you, what sort of thing really irritates you? Can you suggest a punishment for your 'criminals'?

1 I hate people who are more energetic in the morning than I am. People who talk at breakfast, and seem full of fun before 9 o'clock. I'd make them listen to the same joke at breakfast every day!
2 I hate people who don't eat carefully and properly; they use the wrong spoon for the soup, or lean on the table . . . I'd give them a table with all four legs different sizes!
3 I hate people who take longer to prepare for something than they spend doing it – like 2 hours putting on make-up, washing hair, and so on – all for a trip to the cinema. I'd give them a speaking clock which said 'You've been in the bathroom for – minutes' every minute!
4 I hate people who can *do* things – make their own clothes, play the piano, repair their own car, decorate . . . I'd make them watch me do all those jobs – badly!

Group work 10

Read carefully through the descriptions of the following eight people. There are actually four husband-and-wife pairs. See if you can find which man goes with which woman.

A *Martin.* He's 30-year-old and a very successful businessman. He works hard, and for very long hours. He thinks it's very important to get to the top. He's clever, quick, but rather aggressive, and he gets angry very easily.
B *Steve.* He's 27. He was an art student but he's not very successful. His parents were rich, but he doesn't get on well with them and wants to make his own way. He's nice to other people but basically lazy and not very practical.
C *Arnold.* He's 62. He has in fact been married twice before. He has had a very successful career in business – he owns two Rolls Royces at the moment. He's been around the world and done most of the things people want to do. Unfortunately he's not a very happy man. People were rather surprised at his third marriage – two years ago.
D *Ted* is 18. He's a student. His parents are very working class but he is extremely clever and has gone to university very young. He wants to leave his rather unhappy childhood behind him and has tried as hard as possible to 'make the break'. He's basically rather shy and nervous. For this reason people often want to help him. He seems a little helpless on his own.
E *June* is 36. She has a strong personality and has been a successful secretary ever since she left school. She paints in her spare time and enjoys the theatre and music a lot. She had no brothers and sisters and did not marry until she was over 30.

F *Debbie.* She says she's 24 but may perhaps be younger. She was a beauty queen and a very successful one. She is very attractive, very active, she works as a hairdresser — and it's rather obvious, it's her main hobby too. She's not very bright, but it's easy to ignore that when you meet her!

G *Ann* is 27. She is a very successful newspaper reporter. She's confident, aggressive, intelligent, and has a very strong personality. One of her main interests is the role of women in society. She believes women have not had enough opportunities in the past and is doing her best to improve their situation. She impresses everybody as a very strong person.

H *Mary.* She's 31, she was a nurse after she left school but she gave up her job when she got married. Her main interest now is her family. She's a pleasant, gentle, easy-going girl. She is perhaps the happiest of all of them.

Group work 11
Look at the 4 houses on p. 38. Each group should take one and try to write an advert for it. Discuss the advantages. Alternatively, each group can be estate agents and try to sell their house to the others. The others should think of disadvantages.

5 QUESTIONNAIRES

These can be presented as reading comprehension or listening comprehension. Teachers should go through them in advance and make up 'scores' of the following type:

30-40 People like you but find you too dominant. You can be fun but people very easily get tired. Anyway, *why* aren't you a little bit calmer?

Obviously the explanations should be pitched at the level of the class. The questionnaire itself can be photocopied and distributed or simply read out for pupils to write down the appropriate answer — A, B, etc.

1 Are you extrovert?
Answer these questions as honestly as you can and check your rating at the foot of the page. The test is designed to discover which of the two broad psychological types you are — extrovert or introvert. Underline the answer to each of the questions which most closely represents your most usual behaviour or feeling.

1 Do you usually have a quick answer when people talk to you?
a Very much so b Yes c Average d No e Definitely not

2 Are you fond of practical jokes?
a Very much so
b Yes
c Average
d No
e Definitely not

3 Do you dislike doing things which have to be done quickly?
a Very much so b Yes ç Average d No e Definitely not

4 Are you a lively sort of person?
a Very much so
b Yes
c Average
d No
e Definitely not

5 Do you 'look before you leap'?
a Very much so b Yes c Average d No e Definitely not

6 Can you get a party going?
a Very much so
b Yes
c Average
d No
e Definitely not

7 Do you like telling funny stories or jokes?
a Very much so   b Yes   c Average   d No   e Definitely not

8 Do you dislike spicy foods?
a Very much so
b Yes
c Average
d No
e Definitely not

9 Are you rather careless?
a Very much so   b Yes   c Average   d No   e Definitely not

10 Do you tend towards pessimism rather than optimism?
a Very much so   b Yes   c Average   d No   e Definitely not

11 When someone shouts at you do you shout back?
a Very much so   b Yes   c Average   d No   e Definitely not

12 Do you prefer thought to action?
a Very much so
b Yes
c Average
d No
e Definitely not

13 Are you rather impulsive?
a Very much so   b Yes   c Average   d No   e Definitely not

14 Do you tend to avoid meeting new people?
a Very much so
b Yes
c Average
d No
e Definitely not

15 Do you tend to make careful plans in advance?
a Very much so   b Yes   c Average   d No   e Definitely not

2 Will you get an invitation?
Everybody likes going to parties, but parties are only successful if the right people are there. Are *you* one of the right people? Do people want you at their party? Find out by answering these questions. Pick the answer you think is nearest to your view.

1 *Who will you spend the evening talking to?*
  A The person who invited you to the party.
  B As many people as possible.
  C The girl/boy you went with.
  D The tall, brown-eyed, dark-haired really attractive boy/girl you noticed at another party last week.

2 *It's a fancy dress party and lots of your school friends will be there. Who will you go as?*
  A Napoleon.
  B A baby.
  C Marlene Dietrich.
  D An African belly dancer.

3 *When do you leave the party?*
  A 10 o'clock sharp!
  B Just after everybody else has gone.

  C As soon as the beautiful dark-haired girl/boy you were hoping to meet has left.
  D When you see the sun coming up.

4 *At last you've met the girl/boy you were hoping would be at the party. How do you start your conversation?*
  A Where've you been all my life?
  B Excuse me, do you know where the loo is please?
  C Do you like dancing?
  D I collect stamps, what is your hobby?

5 *Someone has just picked up their drink. They trip up and it goes all over you. What do you do?*
  A Pour your drink all over them.
  B Shout at them and call them an idiot.
  C Say it doesn't matter.
  D Just give them a dreadful look and don't speak to them for the rest of the evening.

6 *Somebody you really do NOT like comes to talk to you. Do you:*
  A Talk to them politely so you don't upset anybody else.
  B Say 'Go away, I don't want to talk to you'.

C Try to introduce them to someone else.
D Go to the loo.

7 *You are asked what kind of music you would like to hear:*
A Something loud and fast that you can dance to.
B Something quiet and slow that you can dance to.
C Folk songs so that everyone can sing together.
D Some Chopin so that you can hear each other speak.

8 *While you are dancing to the very fast music, your partner's jeans start to split down the back. What do you do?*
A Say something immediately and help your partner out of the room.
B Wink to the others, but don't tell her/him.
C Start laughing out loud and point so that everyone looks.
D Ignore it completely and wait for someone else to start laughing.

3 Are you a good citizen?
Life if so much nicer if everyone tries to take a positive part. What about you, do you help other people or not? Here is a questionnaire to help you find out.

1 *You see a blind person at the edge of the road. Do you:*
A Ignore him.
B Insist on taking him across the road — even if he says 'It's all right, I can manage thank you'.
C Offer to help, but leave him if he says 'I can manage'.
D Take him across the road and continue with him to wherever he's going.

2 *You see a £10 note lying in the road. Do you:*
A Pick it up and put it in your pocket.
B Take it into the nearest shop and leave it there.
C Take it to the police station.
D Rush up to the nearest person and ask them if they've dropped it.

3 *You see a 3-year-old boy crying in the street. Do you:*
A Walk past.
B Phone the police.
C Go and try to talk to him.
D Go and give him a big cuddle.

4 *Your neighbours are moving. Do you:*
A Take the day off work to help.
B Make sure you're out the day that they move.
C Leave them to do the job themselves but make them pots of tea.
D Get some friends together and all help to carry all the heavy things.

5 *You have just started work. Somebody who has worked for the same organisation for 25 years is leaving. Do you:*
A Organise a collection for a present.
B Give a very small donation when somebody asks you to help buy a present.
C Say 'But I don't know them'.
D Go and explain that you're not giving anything to their present because you don't know them.

6 *You see two teenage boys making fun of an old lady on the bus or train. Do you:*
A Go and tell them to keep quiet.
B Look out of the window and pretend nothing's happening.
C Try and get an adult to go and do something.
D Wait until the boys get off the bus and then go and talk to the old lady.

7 *A friend of yours who smokes a lot goes to a party. You know that the people giving the party don't like smoking. Do you:*
A Tell the friend before he goes that he mustn't smoke.
B Stop him when he takes his cigarettes out at the party.
C Let him do what he wants — it's nothing to do with you.
D Apologise for your friend but don't stop him smoking.

4 Order a friend

Nowadays there are lots of computer services which allow you to write in and say what sort of person you'd like to meet. Here is a simple form to help you to choose your boyfriend/girlfriend.

Put X against any quality you particularly want them to have and O against anything you definitely do not want them to have.

Personality	*Height*
Generous	Very tall
Sensitive	Tall
Tough	Medium
Intelligent	Short
Lively	
	Build
Interests	Heavy and strong
Sport	Medium build
Reading	Slim
Music	
Dancing	*Hair*
The countryside	Dark
	Fair
	Red

Write one sentence which starts 'I'd like someone who is . . .'

Computer Test. This sample test can be used with your pupils or any other similar test that you may find.

WANTED: 1,000 UNMARRIED READERS

Free computer test to find your perfect partner

If you're sixteen or over you can take advantage of this unique test, offered to you by Dateline Europe's largest computer dating organisation.
Just tell us what you're like and what you want, and our computer will find the perfect partner for you absolutely free!
Within a few days of sending in this free test you will receive the computer's description of your perfect partner.

Your Age:................ Your Sex:..........
Height: ....
Colouring: ....
Race/Nationality:................................
Religion: ....

Occupation:...
Christian Name:..................................
Surname:..
Address: ....
....

Using modern psychology, sociology and computer sciences the computer will meticulously compare your personality profile with those of over 60,000 people, detail by detail. Only then will the computer print out a comprehensive and objective description of its choice of the perfect partner for you.
And . . . our superb 36 page full colour brochure.

Do you consider yourself:		Do you like:	
Shy:	☐	Cinema/theatre:	☐
Extrovert:	☐	Good Food:	☐
Adventurous:	☐	Travel:	☐
Family type:	☐	Political Activities:	☐
Clothes-conscious:	☐	Classical music/literature:	☐
Generous:	☐	The Pop scene:	☐
Outdoor type:	☐	Sport:	☐
Creative:	☐	Do-it-yourself:	☐
Practical:	☐	Camping/hiking/climbing:	☐
Intellectual:	☐	Voluntary work:	☐

6 ROLE PLAYS

These are somewhat more difficult and pupils will require some time to prepare their roles. They will be best used with smaller groups of older pupils.

1 A family problem

Sandra Collins is 19. She is very keen to become an artist. She applied while she was at school to go to Art College, but was turned down. She has been working in a shop for the last six months and finds it very dull. Just after she started at the shop she met Roger. He is a junior sales representative for a nationwide firm. They have been going out regularly for the past six months. Her father does not like Roger. He thinks he is just playing around with his daughter.

Yesterday Roger heard that he had been offered a new job with the firm in the north of England. He has been offered a very large increase of salary to become chief sales representative for a small new area. He is delighted to have such a good opportunity while he is so young. (He is 26.) He told Sandra and he wants her to go with him – but he is not prepared to get married yet because he thinks Sandra is too young.

This morning Sandra has got a letter from an Art College saying that they will give her a place from the beginning of the new term. She had almost forgotten this application, but now has a chance to follow her ambition. Unfortunately, the College is in the south-west of England and so she would not be able to see very much of Roger.

Take the part of one of the following people: *Sandra, Roger, Sandra's father, Sandra's mother* (she got married when she was very young herself and regrets this. She thinks she missed a lot in life because she got married so young), *Eileen*, Sandra's older sister. She is 27 and unmarried and likes Roger very much herself.

2 The sports centre

You are on the committee of the local sports centre. A wealthy local has just died and left £40,000 to the centre. The committee has to decide how the money will be spent. The members are:

George Andrews   a local headmaster. He wants the school's football pitches to be improved. He has worked at the same school all his life and is very proud of it. He is also mad about football and thinks everyone else should be too.

Mary Black   doesn't like Mr Andrews. He will not allow Miss Black and the Ladies Badminton Club to use the school gymnasium to practise. Mary needs the money to buy new equipment and to pay the rent for the hall which the club uses. If she doesn't get the money her club will have to close.

Bob Dobbs   is a boxer. He believes all young boys should learn how to fight. He thinks all other sports are for girls. Only boxing is a proper 'man's' sport. He argues with everybody.

Sam Sned   is a member of the local golf club. To him golf is the most civilised of all sports, where you can meet nice people. He thinks all young boys should be given the chance to play golf as young as possible. He wants the money to be spent on setting up a junior golf club for boys between 10 and 16. He does not want girl members.

Ann Brown   is very annoyed because everyone wants the money to go to boys' sports. She thinks all young girls should learn to ride. She wants to set up a Girls' Riding Club. She would use the money to buy two horses and rent stables. She herself has a horse, and believes in Women's Lib.

Rev. Peacock   runs the local Boy Scouts. He tries not to disagree with anyone and tries to calm everyone down. But he would like some of the money for his Scouts who want to go to Norway next summer to camp.

Major Chalmers   is the chairman of the local Hunting Club. When his members go out hunting foxes they do a lot of damage to farmers' fences. His club is famous in the area and it needs this money to pay for the damage. They also need new guns.

Chairman, Mr Edward Gray   tries to encourage everyone to say what they think but *he* believes the money should be used for quiet, indoor games like chess, darts and so on.

3 Improving the town

You are members of a committee. You have only £6m to spend on improvements to your town. The committee has to decide at a meeting how the money should be used over the next few years. There are several suggestions, together with their costs which are going to be considered. You only have money for half these suggestions.

1)	To build a ring road round the town to take all traffic away from the centre.	£2m
2)	To build a new town hall in the city centre.	£2m
3)	To build two large multi-storey car parks near the shopping centre.	£½m
4)	To make a large area of the town a pedestrian precinct.	£½m
5)	To put bus shelters in the suburbs where people often have to wait a long time for a bus.	£½m
6)	To build an indoor swimming pool.	£1½m
7)	Employ more staff to keep the town centre tidier.	£2m
8)	Provide independent shopping advice centre.	£1m
9)	Build a new youth centre.	£1m
10)	Build a roller-skating centre.	£1m

Arnold Seddon
You are only interested in one thing – sport – and you don't mind what happens providing the swimming pool is part of the scheme which is accepted.

Bernard Bottomly
You are an ex-army officer and you were elected to the Committee because you were strongly against private cars. You are used to telling people what to do without discussing. You are very aggressive.

Lilian Chumley
Your special interests are in the housewives and the suburbs. You get very annoyed if people argue for more things for children.

Sidney Basing-Stoker
You are not interested in how the money is spent, but you like people to discuss things calmly and quietly. You never lose your temper and you try to make everybody else quieter.

Christine Booth
You are particularly interested in good facilities for children. You want all the improvements to show a real interest in children. You always disagree at meetings with Mrs Chumley.

Angela Dickens
You think that the town used to be more impressive and important but not enough has been done to make it 'a nice place to live'. You used to live in a bigger and more important town and you want your little town to impress your friends when they visit you.

Now act out a meeting. You must put the views given above and you must have the sort of personality suggested for you. After the discussions the Committee will vote on how the money is going to be spent.

7 THE AGONY COLUMN

Dear Sylvia,
Two years ago my grandfather died and my grandmother came to live with us. At first it was fun because she was always giving me small presents, but now she won't leave me alone. She keeps asking about everything I've been doing and always wants me to do jobs for her, running to the shops and so on. I like my gran but she is becoming an awful nuisance. How can I tell her?
'Friendly and 14'

Dear friendly,
You say you are friendly but you don't seem it to me. It sounds to me as if you're being rather mean. When you were getting something out of gran it was all right, but when she expects something back you don't like it at all. I think

perhaps you ought to learn to be a little bit more generous towards other people.

Dear Sylvia,
I am just 15 and have moved into a room of my own at home. The other night I invited some of my friends round to listen to some records, but my father was furious when he found us alone in the room and made us come down to the sitting room. He has told me I am not allowed to have any of my friends in my room without him or my mother being there.
'Embarrassed'

Dear embarrassed,
Your father is obviously worried about you. I am sure he only wants to help. The best thing is to ask one or two of your friends who have rooms of their own what their parents do and then perhaps to ask them if their parents could have a word with your Dad. Try not to get upset. He's only trying to help. It's probably best if you take your friends into the sitting room first and then say, 'Do you mind if we go to my room for a while now'. Then he probably won't worry so much.

Dear Sylvia,
I am 18 and going out with a boy I like very much. The other day we went for a drink in the pub; he had some beer and I had a grapefruit juice. Then six friends of his who he plays football with turned up, and one of them bought us both a drink. After they'd gone, he said that he hoped I would offer to buy a round sometimes too, and not just expect the boys to pay all the time. This seemed very mean to me. Do you think I should pay?
'Silent partner'

Dear silent partner,
I agree with your boyfriend. You are very lucky to have found a boy who is prepared to take a girl as an equal and you should do what you can to keep him, even if it sometimes costs you some money.

3.9 Discussion items

The following short articles or extracts all appeared in English newspapers recently. They should all be a suitable peg on which to hang a discussion; notice that they are short and suggest an obvious discussion point. Time should not be spent wading through the text in class, it's sufficient for the pupils to read the text quickly, or even for you to read it aloud for them; it is to form the basis of a discussion, not to swamp the lesson. This selection is to show you the sort of items which are usually successful. In some cases, discussion questions have been added.

The baddies

☐ not only smoke but offer cigarettes to other people.
☐ press drinks or food on someone.
☐ stock up on duty-free cigarettes and alcohol.
☐ use lifts and escalators.
☐ eat a big lunch even when there's a dinner party planned for the evening.
☐ give sweets to other people's children.
☐ smoke without permission at table or in other people's cars and houses.
☐ let smoke drift into someone else's face.
☐ sympathise or agree with people who say they just can't stop smoking or lose weight.
☐ coo over bonny babies.
☐ don't bother with seat belts on short journeys.
☐ skimp breakfast and eat snacks all morning.
☐ play transistor radios in public.

The goodies

☐ offer to do someone's car seat belt for them and won't take no for an answer.
☐ host parties which offer non-alcoholic drinks and lots of food as well as booze.
☐ don't smoke.
☐ provide a substantial salad or other healthy options for slimmers at dinner parties.
☐ compliment people on losing weight.
☐ stay away from work and

parties if suffering from a bad cold or flu.

☐ make it easy for a driver not to drink by offering alternatives.

☐ meet friends for lunch at a gym or swimming pool rather than the pub.

☐ get up early for a jog.

☐ eat lots of fish and vegetables.

☐ drink alcohol only at mealtimes.

☐ walk or cycle rather than using the car.

Who are your goodies and baddies?

Life 'Too Quiet' for Millionaire

The former footballer who built up a 49-store super-market chain before selling it for £3,750,000 has been driven back into business after just eight months by boredom, according to his son, Kevin, 25.

Asked why, he said 'I've never done nothing, and I'm not starting now.'

Pet 'Better than watch on Retirement'

A pet was a more appropriate present for anyone retiring than a gold watch.

Animals not only provided companionship for an old person living alone but gave security and, in many instances, led to a more fulfilling retirement.

The association, which condemned the ruling by many local authorities that pets must not be kept in rented houses or flats, said the keeping of a pet often motivated the senior members of the community to go out to shop for food, thereby also encouraging them to eat and make provisions for adequate heating at home.

Animals can be wonderful company.

Certainly, for people who can't make friends with other people – animals don't answer back.

What do you think?

Teach drinking at home – plea to parents

Young people should be taught to drink wisely at home, the National Council on Alcoholism advises today. Even teetotal parents ought to consider introducing their children to drink at home, the council says in its annual report.

'Young people should neither have their first experience nor acquire their later drinking habits from outside home.

'It should be under the home influence that young people learn to appreciate the use of alcohol.'

'The desire of those parents who wish to bring their children up in an alcohol-free environment must be respected, but teetotal parents must recognise that in our present culture and environment their children will be confronted with alcohol and a personal decision about its use,' continues the report.

It certainly cannot be taken for granted that children will accept their parents' views, the report says.

'In fact it is more likely that they will react against them.'

Would you teach your children to drink at home?

What about smoking?

Is it better to be strict and stop your children doing things like that, or to encourage them to try while you're there to keep an eye on them?

Hairdressing ban in Iran

Male hairdressers in Iran have been ordered to stop cutting women's hair and women will no longer be allowed to cut men's hair. The Central Revolutionary Committee, which has also outlawed blow waves and setting, says the practices are against the Islamic moral code.

Would you be willing to work in a country which has social customs so very different from your own?

Have you ever visited a 'foreign' foreign country?

Headlines

Newspaper headlines have a peculiar style of their own. So much is omitted that you can be in considerable doubt as to what you are going to read beneath them. What do you think these articles are about and can you express them in more everyday words?

1 Egg talks broken off
2 Cloud bursts over Sunny Jim
3 Water board under fire
4 Crowd shouts for death as murderer given life
5 Police anger as Constable bought for nation
6 PM stuck in jam
7 Broom brushes off injury to sweep board
8 Minister slams door on union
9 Police detain man in Moors case
10 Airgun ban urged
11 Plot alleged by Crown
12 Pay deal shelved
13 Axed boss hits back
14 Flu sweeps London
15 Pay row hits press
16 Export clamp by Japan
17 Pensions swindler reported
18 Minister in quandary over fish talks

Symbols

Can you say the following sentences aloud? (You have to say any symbols that appear too.)
1 There was a 10% increase in prices last year.
2 He lived there 1923-31.
3 The latest opinion poll gives Labour 39.4% support.
4 These rings are 5cm x 0.005cm.
5 Schoolteachers often get 'annoyed'.
6 Dear Sir/Madam.
7 Some people (particularly young people) think things should be changed.
8 It's about ¾ mile from here.
9 The conference starts 30.6.79.
10 It cost exactly £3.25.
11 Water freezes at 0°C.
12 It was very cold yesterday, −3°.
13 5 x 4 = 20.
14 The speed limit on the motorways is 70 mph (about 110 kmh).
15 Questions marked * are to be answered by men only, those marked † by women only.
16 Mark the statements you agree with ✓, if you disagree, mark with an X.
17 At present rates $2.38 = £1.
18 I need some 2″ screws.
19 The 4.38 am train has just arrived.
20 At last!!!

3.10   Five-minute fillers

Every teacher knows how useful it is to have something 'in your back pocket' to fill up five minutes at the end of a lesson, or at some other point when perhaps part of the class is not present, or whatever. Here are a number of ideas, mostly for younger pupils, for these 'five-minute fillers'.

(a) Hangman

This is a popular game in language classes but remember it does generate relatively little language. You can improve it by insisting pupils use the phrase 'Is there . . . in it please?', rather than just calling out letters.

(b) I spy

The verb *spy* is of course rather unusual. Change the traditional game to make it more useful in the language classroom by using, for example,

I've just seen something beginning with . . .
I can see something beginning with . . .

(c) Prefixes

Write a number of words on the board with their first two letters missing. Pupils have to produce *any* word which ends with the letters you've given, eg if you put TLAW they can add OU.

This can be a good deal more difficult than

you would expect. Here are some examples you may like to use:

RPT	VEL	ANGES	EW
LEEP	URCH	TROL	READY
USE	INK	TTY	ONG
OOR	UNG	OON	AIN
OWER	OTES	ILET	EEL

It's a good idea to use words that pupils have had trouble remembering or have had difficulty in saying in an earlier lesson.

(d) Jumbled letters
Write on the board groups of letters with a theme, but jumble the letters of the words. Here, for example, are different kinds of animals:

Epseh lahew resho xof rabe taplehen
nilo regit wco orgakona nerederi anesk
gfor myneko ogd emuso nomwa

But remember, it can be made more difficult by using adjectives, or words you had in an earlier lesson, and so on.

(e) Making words
The teacher writes a longish word on the blackboard and individuals or groups are given a few minutes to write down as many new words as possible using only the letters of the word on the board. The group/individual with the most wins. (Obviously it's best to include common letters in your word if you want to make it easier for younger pupils. Try, for example, teacher, English, Christmas, stranger, television.)

(f) Odd rhymes
Put a number of words on the board with similar sounds in them. All the words rhyme except one. The students identify the odd one out.

The next two fillers are slightly more difficult and are more useful for intermediate or advanced classes.

(g) Abbreviations
Put four or five common abbreviations on the board. Ask pupils for their meaning. Do *not* use things like OBE, but rather the practical abbreviations you find in classified ads., cinema adverts and so on.

(h) Tongue Twisters
A tongue twister will always fill a few minutes, but remember that it is better to use one based on the particular problems of English for speakers of (French), rather than a normal native speaker problem. One such, however, can always be used to amuse younger classes – *red lorry, yellow lorry*. Introduce as follows:

'Can you say this (put *red* on blackboard) and this (put *yellow* on blackboard under *red*) and this (put *lorry* on the blackboard – draw it if they don't understand the word). Now, if anyone can say *red lorry, yellow lorry*, three times without a mistake and without a pause, you can finish five minutes early.'

Result – someone can and you let them go early, or, much more likely, no-one can and it takes five minutes for everyone to try!

3.11 Literature

You may be teaching the oldest and most able pupils who are reading some work of English Literature from a literary point of view. If you have read and know something about the work, or are interested in any way, you may find it possible to have a discussion with them about it and get them to tell you something about a work in their own language that they have read and enjoyed. This of course will involve co-operation with the native teacher. You may also find that it is possible to co-operate with teachers other than the English teacher – for example, the history teacher may be doing something about England which you yourself have studied and are interested in. In the same way, if you have other interests you may find it possible to connect what you do to what is happening in your pupils' ordinary lessons in some other subject. This, however, is obviously going to be true only for those working with pupils at the upper end of the secondary school.

Chapter 4

Teaching Materials — 3

In this section we suggest a number of rather unconventional ideas for language teaching materials. Primarily they are games or light-hearted activities, but each of them has a serious language teaching point embedded (and sometimes concealed) within it. The aim is to make the pupils use language of which they are often unaware and which is frequently a very long way from the obvious use of these exercises. In each case we comment briefly on the language you can expect and why.

If these activities are to be successful they must be conducted mainly, or ideally exclusively, in English. It is the language around the activity rather than the activity itself that is the object of these materials. It is therefore most important that you have made clear to the pupils that they must speak English and that you yourself will only speak in English.

4.1 Conversation-building activities

In addition to the traditional conversation lesson, based on a topic, there are a number of ways of giving the outline of a conversation (often very short) which the pupils then build either as a class or, more frequently, in pairs into a full natural exchange.

THE CLOZE DIALOGUE

The pupils are given a dialogue written out on stencil, overhead transparency or the blackboard, from which certain key words have been deleted. The number and choice of such words of course depends on the class. They read the dialogue in pairs adding suitable words to the gaps. In some cases there will only be a single word which will be appropriate in the gap, while in others a choice may be available.

Permission

A: . . . you . . . . . . I smoke?
B: I'd . . . you . . . . I'm afraid I've got . . . a bad . . . at . . . .
A: Oh fine.
  (a short time later)
B: . . . . . ., . . . I open the window, ... I'm not feeling very well.
A: Yes of course. . . . you mind . . . I looked at your paper for a moment.
B: No that's . . . .
A: . . . very much.
B: . . . . keeping an eye on my bag for a moment, please?
A: With . . . .

Leaving

A: What time . . . . it, Jill?
B: . . . about ten to.
A: . . .?
B: No, ten to twelve.
A: . . ., is it as late as that? We really . . . . . . be going.
C: . . .? Would . . . . . . a cup of . . . before you . . . .
A: . . . . The last bus goes . . . a few minutes. I think we'd . . . go . . . .
C: Well, it's been . . . seeing you again. I hope we . . . meet again . . . .
A: Yes, that . . . be nice, but you . . . come . . . to us next time.
C: Oh thanks . . .'d be . . . .
A: . . ., we'll . . . . . . be . . . . Thanks again.

An invitation

A: . . . . . . going out this evening?
B: That'd be . . . .

A: Is there anywhere you'd . . . .
. . . .
B: No no, I'll . . . it to you.
A: . . . . . .?
B: Well I think I'd . . . go for . . . to eat, if . . .
. . . .
A: Fine. That . . . me.

(Notice you have to decide in advance if you are going to treat items like *don't* and *it'd* as one or two items. We prefer to treat them as single items.)

THE INFORMATION-ONLY DIALOGUE

Similar to the cloze dialogue, except all non-information words (please, excuse me, I'm afraid, etc.) are omitted and only the bare outline of what the speakers mean is left. This is much more difficult than the cloze dialogue, however. You will usually need to discuss it line by line with the class before asking them to read it naturally in pairs. If you write these yourself you should include the minimum information possible and, of course, choose situations in which the pupils may want to use their English themselves.

Dialogue 1

Charles wants a *Daily Telegraph*. He's in the newsagent's.

Charles: *The Daily Telegraph*.
Woman: There's none left.
Charles: What else have you got?
Woman: *The Times* and *The Mirror*.
Charles: *The Times*.
Woman: 20p.
Charles: (*Gives her a £5 note*) I've no change.
Woman: I can't change that.
Charles: Oh, where can I get it changed?
Woman: I don't know.
Customer: There's a bank on the corner.
Charles: Oh! (*He turns to leave and bumps into a woman with a baby. He goes out.*)

Dialogue 2

Jack is at the railway station.

Man: Yes?
Jack: I want to go to London.
Man: What sort of ticket do you want?
Jack: A return.
Man: Are you going now?
Jack: Yes.
Man: Are you coming back today?
Jack: Yes.
Man: Four pounds fifty.
Jack: When is the next train?
Man: I don't know. Ask at the information office.

Situations suitable for information only dialogues include: *Buying* – tickets, something in shops; *Getting information* – at the information bureau, bank, railway station, from a stranger in the street; *At home* – dialogue at breakfast, over a meal, about a television programme you're watching, when offered something, etc.

THE SKELETON DIALOGUE

This is ideally done on the blackboard. A complete dialogue is presented and then particular items removed successively as different pairs in the class read. As you remove items the pupils are allowed to continue using the dialogue verbatim or they may vary the items you have rubbed out.

Presented as a skeleton initially these dialogues are one of the main ways of providing a framework for a very weak class to ensure that they at least say *something*.

Conversation 1
A: Hello, H. . . . .?
B: . . ., ... And . . . .?
A: Not . . . . . ., ... I haven't s. . . . . .
. . . .
. . . . since I last saw you?
B: Oh, nothing much, ...?

Conversation 2
A: Hello. H. . . . .?

B: . . . . . ., . . . y. . . . H. . . . .?
A: F. . . t. . . . It's . . . b. . . m. . ., ...
B: L. . ., isn't it? I haven't seen you for . . . a
. . . time.

Conversation 3
You: I'd . . . a ticket to London, ...
Clerk: . . . or return?
You: A day . . ., ...
Clerk: . . . or . . . class?
You: S. . . class, ...
Clerk: That'll be £2.85, please.
You: Thank . . . . When does the
3 o'clock . . . in, . . .?
Clerk: Oh, about 3.55 I think.
You: . . . .

COMPLETING THE STORY

The teacher tells a story which is contrived so
that he describes but does not produce the
language needed for various speech events. The
pupils are required to fill in what the characters
in the story say at the points where the teacher
pauses. In most cases only one phrase is exactly
right.

(a) Mrs Rogers was rather old. She found it
difficult to hurry and when she got to the
station it was late. She wasn't sure where
to get the train so she asked *(1)* . . . The
man told her it was platform 7. She was
struggling with her bag when a young man
said, *(2)* . . . She thanked him and he took
her case and put it on the train for her.
The train was very crowded. The young
man saw two empty seats so he asked a
man sitting nearby *(3)* . . . The man said
'No' so John took one of the seats and
Mrs Rogers the other. She thanked the
young man for helping with her bag *(4)*
. . . he answered. It was very warm on the
train and the man sitting beside Mrs
Rogers asked *(5)* . . . Mrs Rogers said
'No' so he opened the window. The young
man took out his cigarettes but the other
man said *(6)* . . . The young man, who

hadn't noticed, said *(7)* . . . and put the
cigarettes in his pocket again. Then he
decided to go for a cup of coffee. He
offered to bring Mrs Rogers one but she
wasn't thirsty so she said *(8)* . . . It was so
crowded the young man thought he might
lose his seat while he was away so he
asked Mrs Rogers *(9)* . . . *(10)* . . . she said
and the young man went to the buffet car.
Mrs Rogers was nervous. She didn't often
travel on trains. She asked the man *(11)*
. . . He told her he thought it was about
two hours. Then he took a timetable out
of his pocket *(12)* . . . he said. 'Oh thank
you very much,' Mrs Rogers said.
Suddenly the train stopped. The man
looked out of the window *(13)* . . . asked
Mrs Rogers. 'There's something on the
line,' the man told her. I can't see what it
is but it looks like . . . .

(b) It was dark and it was late. Jack was
standing at the bus stop. A man came up
to him. He had an unlit cigarette in his
mouth *(1)* . . . he asked, rather aggressively. Jack felt in his pockets but he had
no matches *(2)* . . . he said. *(3)* . . . asked
the man even more aggressively. Jack,
who didn't know that part of the town at
all well, said *(4)* . . . He tried to be
pleasant but the man seemed very odd *(5)*
. . . he asked. 'About five to twelve,' Jack
told him. 'There's a bus in a few minutes.'
'Is there? Well you're not going on the
bus. You're coming with me,' said the
man. *(6)* . . . asked Jack. 'I said you're
coming with me,' said the man, taking
hold of Jack's arm. *(7)* . . . shouted Jack
angrily. *(8)* . . . 'And I'll hurt you more if
you don't keep quiet,' the man said.
Suddenly a car swung into the road. It
was driving very fast. It stopped just
beside Jack and the man. Someone
wound the window down *(9)* . . . the
driver said. *(10)* . . . shouted Jack. But,
although he struggled furiously the man
pushed him into the car . . . .

(In addition to supplying the missing items here pupils can be encouraged to continue or complete the stories.)

DIALOGUE BUILDING

The pupils in pairs are given a short description of 'who they are' and the first two or three lines of a dialogue. They may be given one or two pieces of simple information which are required to complete the dialogue. These speech events are nearly always of the kind between two strangers, and the whole event will only be five or six lines long (ie they are 'tourist situations').

(a) A has been visiting B for a meal. A is about to leave.
B: Well, it was so nice to see you again. I'm glad you could come round.
A:

(b) A and B are friends. They haven't met for a while. A had an accident recently but B doesn't know about it.
A: Hello, how are you?
B:
A: Not too bad, thanks. As a matter of fact I had a bit of a smash yesterday.
B:
A:

(etc.)

(c) A and B, who do not know each other, are sitting opposite each other on the train.
A: Excuse me, I think you've spilt some coffee on your dress.
B:

(d) A and B are on the train. They do not know each other.
A: Excuse me I'm afraid I can't get through because of your bags.
B:

(e) A and B are friends. They're planning an evening out together.
A:
B: Tuesday? I'm afraid I can't make Tuesday. I'm playing tennis.
A:
B:

A: Yes, that'll be fine. What time shall we say?

(f) A and B are having a meal in a restaurant.
A: This is very nice, isn't it?
B:
A: That's David over there, isn't it?
B:
A: Oh you're quite right. I was mistaken.
C: May I? (reaches for the pepper and salt).
B:
A:

(g) B and C are friends of A's. B does not know C.
A: I don't think you two have met before have you.
B:
C:

(h) A and B do not know each other. A phones to speak to B's son, Dennis. B is at home on his own.
A: Oh good evening, could I speak to Dennis please.
B:

(i) A is a teenager who is visiting a friend, B. C, who is B's mother, has given them coffee and biscuits.
B: Oh be careful! Oh dear, now you've spilt tea everywhere.
A:
C:

INFORMATION GAP SITUATIONS

This heading covers a very wide range of similar activities but varying from the very simple to activities suitable for the most advanced classes. The basic principle is that a single pupil, a group of pupils or the class want a piece of information that only one pupil or a small group in the class has got. At its simplest level this is the *Who am I?* game (see p. 35). At its most advanced level it could be used to teach a class of pupils studying, say, physics in their final year at school. One pupil goes to the library to look up some information about a topic in physics which pupils are studying in their other classes. The others then cross-question him about the information so that they too can make use of it.

In a case like this the ideal is to give different pupils different tasks so that at the end of the lesson the class will have a complete picture of the subject matter of something they are studying in one of their other lessons. This obviously requires your co-operation with other members of staff (not just the English teacher), but will often ensuré the classes are highly motivated and have a real purpose for using their English.

This is also a useful principle with younger classes when your host colleagues ask you to talk about the British education system. Rather than giving a talk, suggest to the teacher that the class prepares questions to ask you. This will clearly ensure that the information is of the kind he expects them to have and they control the level of what you say, thereby preventing you talking a long way above their heads.

The most typical information gap situations, however, are when you have planned the gap in advance. This means giving different pupils different information, perhaps written out on cards, and can be as simple as a set of three cards saying as follows:

1   *You want to make a phone call; you have no coins, only a pound note*
2   *You have no money with you*
3   *You have lots of change in your pocket*

Notice there are no instructions and the first pupil does not know whether to ask *2* or *3*. If he asks *2* he will obviously have to decline, then *3* may offer help. Alternatively, *1* may have to ask *3* too; or he may begin by asking *3* in which case *2* has no role at all.

We suggest in chapter 7 that you take with you a number of sources of information (brochures, entertainment guides from the newspapers, etc.). Obviously these are ideal for information gap activities. One pupil is given the timetable or brochure and the others have to get the information from him. Remember, this will be excellent practice for any student who wants to use his English in England as this

is a situation in which he will frequently find himself.

Perhaps the most effective of all information gap activities are those that arise from the pupils' own interests. If, for example, one pupil can play a particular game, then the gap arises naturally since he knows something they do not but need to. Clearly, however, you will be needed to make sure that the interchange takes place in English.

It must be obvious that people very often ask their students 'What did you do at the weekend?'. This is an information gap – nobody else knows – but it is hardly of any great interest. It makes a good deal more sense to ask 'What are you going to do this weekend?'; then, if a pupil knows about some local event or whatever and the others express interest, you have a natural information gap activity. The importance of you exploiting these opportunities cannot be over-emphasised.

SITUATIONS

These are the most difficult exercises of this type. A situation, usually involving two or occasionally three speakers, is described verbally to the pupils. They must then try to build the whole conversation that would arise out of the circumstances.

Again, however, these situations can vary from the simple 'you want to find out the time of the last train from London to Brighton, but the person you ask is also a stranger', to a description of a disagreement, argument or formal meeting. Most often they are based on a problem where the two speakers have different information, attitudes or plans, and some sort of solution, compromise or agreement has to be reached.

Situations
(a) What would you say in each of these situations? In most cases there is a particular phrase which is always used. Remember particularly that if you translate what you say in your own language it may sound very odd:

1 An Englishman says to you, 'This is Jill'. You've never met her before. What do you say?

2 The Englishman says, 'You haven't met my grandmother before, have you?' You haven't. What do you say?

3 Mr Rogers says, 'How do you do' to you. What do you answer?

4 What do you say when someone says, 'Hello, how are you?'

5 You're meeting a friend. You're a quarter of an hour late. What do you say?

6 You're sitting on a bus, next to the window. Someone is sitting next to you. You want to get off. What do you say?

7 You meet an acquaintance and ask about a friend of theirs. They tell you the friend has had an accident. What do you say?

8 You help someone to carry a heavy bag. He says, 'Thank you very much'. How do you answer?

9 You don't hear what someone says. You want them to say it again. What do you say?

10 You answer the telephone and give your number. The other person says, 'I'm so sorry, I've got the wrong number'. How do you answer?

11 You're meeting a friend. He arrives late and says, 'I'm so sorry I'm late, I missed the bus'. What do you say?

12 Somebody asks you the time. You haven't got your watch on. What do you say?

13 It's a friend's birthday. What do you say to him?

14 It's the third of January. You meet someone you haven't seen since Christmas. What do you say to them?

15 How do they answer?

16 A friend has just taken his driving test. He's just heard he's passed. What do you say to him?

17 He's just heard he's failed. What do you say to him this time?

18 You're with a friend at home. He says, 'Can you pass me the whatsit please?'. You don't know what he wants. What do you say?

19 You've been visiting a friend for the evening. It's getting late and you think you should be going soon. You want to warn the friend. What do you say?

20 A friend asks to borrow your pen. What do you say as you pass it to him?

21 You pour a cup of coffee for a friend. What do you say when you pass that to him? (Remember, he hasn't asked for it.)

22 You asked a friend to post a letter for you yesterday. You want to check if he really did post it.

23 He forgot! What does *he* say?

24 You have accepted his apology. What do you say?

25 Somebody says 'You're Jack Waters aren't you?' You aren't! What do you say?

(b) These situations, which require more language from the pupils, perhaps in the form of a discussion, argument or conversation, may be done either by describing them to the class and having pupils working in pairs or by writing out the two halves of the situation on cards and giving them to the pairs.

1 A and B are discussing how to spend the evening. A suggests they should both go to the cinema. B wants to save money for her holidays so she suggests they stay at home and listen to some records. A agrees.

2 A and B have just been to the cinema. A is very enthusiastic about the film and especially about the star. B thinks the film was too long and wasn't impressed by the star. They disagree – but in a very pleasant way. 'A starts: *What did you think of that then?*'

3 A is trying to work in the library. B, whom he does not know, is sitting opposite him. A can hear B singing quietly. It's very distracting. He asks B to keep quiet. B apologises and explains he was concentrating so hard on his work that he didn't know he was singing.

4 A and B are friends. They sometimes play tennis together.

A: You are going away with your parents on Friday afternoon this week and won't be back until late on Sunday evening. You're free next weekend, except on Friday when you've promised to visit your grandmother.

B: You ask A to play tennis with you this weekend. You're free all weekend, but Saturday afternoon would suit you best. You can't play next Saturday because you're taking part in a swimming competition, but you are free next Friday and Sunday.

5 A and B are friends. Last year they went on holiday together to Spain because A wanted to. B didn't enjoy Spain very much so this year he wants to choose. B wants to go somewhere warm with a good beach and doesn't want to go in June or July. He thinks it would be best to fly because it's so quick. A can only get his holidays in June or July and thought this year they might take a car so they could visit the countryside.

6 *A*: You've been standing in a shop waiting to be served for five minutes. B comes in and pushes past you and begins to talk to the assistant. Start, 'Excuse me, I think I'm first', then continue.

B: A has been standing in a shop waiting. You are in a terrible hurry to catch a train. You rush in and start to talk to the assistant. A speaks to you but you are in a very bad mood and you just ignore him, at least the first time he speaks.

7 A and B, who do not know each other, are sharing a table in a pizzeria.

A: You want a cigarette before your meal but you have no matches with you. You ask B.

B: You are in the middle of your lunch. You don't smoke and you don't like people who smoke in restaurants − what's more, you always tell them what you think.

8 A wants B to play squash with him on Saturday morning. B has already arranged to play against C at that time. They

arrange to play next Tuesday after school instead. A says he hopes he enjoys the game with C on Saturday.

9 A and B who do not know each other are on a train. A wants to do certain things. B agrees or disagrees politely:

(i) A wants to open the window (B agrees).

(ii) A wants to smoke, although it's a non-smoking compartment (B disagrees).

(iii) A wants to borrow B's newspaper (B agrees).

(iv) A wants to move B's case to make more room for his (B agrees).

10 A and B have met at a party. They didn't know each other before but, of course, they don't want to have an argument. A lives in the middle of a big city and likes living in the city very much. B used to live in town but now lives in a small place in the country and is much happier there. He thinks towns are dirty, noisy and unpleasant. Try to build the conversation they have when A says, 'Which part of town do you live in?'.

11 A and B are two students who are inter-railing. They do not know each other but have been travelling together for three days. They're in Vienna. A has already been to Italy and Greece. B has been in Germany and up to Copenhagen. They both have two more weeks' travelling left. They are trying to decide where to go next and whether to go together or to separate. A starts, 'I think I might go through Nice and Monte Carlo to Marseilles and then on to Spain'.

12 A and B bump into each other in a department store. They apologise, then they look at each other. Each is sure that he has seen the other person before but can't remember where or when. A says, 'Excuse me, haven't we met before?' In fact, they met two years before on a summer holiday/course.

(c) Here the pupils are given only a short

description of the situations. Notice, too, that the number of students who speak in these can vary. They are obviously more difficult than the earlier situations.

1   You are in a train compartment with an elderly woman, a young girl and a tough-looking man of about 20. He starts to chain-smoke Gauloise although it is a non-smoking compartment. The elderly lady asks him to stop but he refuses rudely. Help her.

2   You are travelling by train. You have bought a return ticket (cost £6.50) but when the inspector comes to check it you cannot find it. Try and convince him you are not cheating.

3   You have just finished a meal in a pizzeria. Neither the service nor the food has been very good. When the waiter brings the bill you find there is a mistake in it. Complain and ask for a new bill.

4   You are driving in a strange town and by mistake turn right into a busy road. You did not see the 'no right turn' sign but it *is* clearly visible. A policeman stops you and asks for an explanation. You apologise and make excuses.

5   You are arriving in London at 9 pm by plane and are going to stay with an English friend. Now you learn your plane will be four hours delayed. Phone the friend and explain what is happening.

6   A couple of teenagers in leather jackets and dirty jeans come up to you at a railway station and ask if they could 'borrow' £2 for their fare home. You do not believe they intend to return it to you and you refuse politely but firmly.

7   There are two of you. An English speaking friend (American or English) has asked your advice – what are the possibilities in your country for him to get a job. Advise him.

8   The same friend has asked if you think there is any chance of him being able to study in your country. He's good at maths and chemistry but not very good at foreign languages. He thinks a year in a foreign country would be a big help to him before he goes to study (to be a doctor) in his own country.

9   A friend invited you to a party last Saturday but you couldn't go. You were in a hurry when she asked you and didn't have time to explain why not. The reason was because you already had an invitation to someone else you both know very well, but this other person didn't invite the first friend to her party. Now she's heard about it and is rather upset. She thinks you tried to avoid visiting her and kept the other invitation secret. Another friend has told you she's very upset.

Take the parts of the two students. One telephones the other to clear the air.

10   You're in England. You're going to buy a hamburger. When you see the person in front of you in the queue you see that he gets lots of different 'things' on his hamburger. You order yours with all the extras.

(d)   In each of the following situations you need some piece of authentic material – newspapers, adverts, brochures or, in a few cases, information of the kind which you can compile yourself. In a few cases we give example material but almost invariably these lessons will be more interesting and effective if you produce the real thing.

1   Holiday

Divide the class into pairs. Give one person one of the two holidays described below. It's a holiday for two people. Decide which one you prefer to go on.

Holiday no. 1

A week's trip to New York
By fast comfortable Jumbo Jet

Good-looking hostesses to calm your flying fears and pamper you all the way. All meals, wine, and in-flight cinema included.

Luxury Hotel

Foreign language guide available 24 hours a day. Guided tours every day. Your every need taken care of. Just say what you want and we do it.
That's our motto.

Americo Tours

Holiday no. 2

A week in England

Travel the human way by luxury coach and ultra-modern boat.

Dancing, casinos, cinema on board: just like an ocean liner. And then a week in REAL England. The Lake District, the best scenery in England. The nicest people. Staying at small hotels off the beaten track.

Tours arranged, but self-drive cars available. Hill-walking if that's what you like. Picturesque villages to wander around at your own speed.
Get away from the rush.

Anglo Tours

2   Arriving in London
Work in pairs. Two of you are travelling on a cold, wet January day with a lot of luggage to Victoria. You come through the customs at Heathrow at half past two. A friend is meeting you at Victoria at 6.15 to catch the 6.25 train. Discuss the best way to get to Victoria. Here is the information you'll need:

If you arrive at Heathrow airport there are two common ways of travelling into town — bus and tube. There are advantages to both, the tube is direct to the centre of town, but if you want to go, for example, to Victoria station you have to change, either across the platform in the open air or with quite a long underground walk nearer the town centre. If you take the bus it leaves you at the Cromwell Road terminal, two hundred metres from the nearest tube, and often there is a long queue for taxis. Although bus and tube cost about the same (bus is a little more) taxis are, of course, relatively expensive. The tubes go regularly every quarter of an hour at peak times, the buses are every ten minutes and have a special trailer for luggage. Unfortunately the bus route is into London

along the M4, and at morning and evening rush hours the 40 minute journey can take well over an hour. The tube regularly takes 40 minutes.

3   Arranging to meet
Look at the timetable and advert. You are staying in Brighton. You plan to go to the Saturday matinee with a friend who lives in a London suburb. You'd like to have something to eat with the friend — either lunch before you go to the theatre, or something to eat afterwards. You don't want to get home after ten o'clock, though, because you're expecting a phone call from your family. Discuss the arrangements with your friend.

Brighton — London
Mondays to Saturdays

		East	
	Brighton	Croydon	Victoria
	dep.	arr.	arr.
SX	08.18	09.03	09.20
SX	08.35 C	09.22	09.39
SO	08.37 D	09.18	09.33
	09.00 D	09.52	10.08
SX	09.20	10.05	10.20
	09.37 E	10.18	10.33
	then at the following		
	minutes past each hour		
	00 C	52	08
	37 C	18	33
	until		
	16.00 E	16.52	17.11 C
	16.37 C	17.18	17.30
	17.00 E	17.52	18.11 C

SO – Saturdays only
SX – Saturdays excepted

London — Brighton
Mondays to Saturdays

	East	
Victoria	Croydon	Brighton
dep.	dep.	arr.
16.10 E	16.25	17.05

SX	16.30 C	16.47	17.36
SO	16.40	16.55	17.47
SX	16.55 B	17.10	17.57
SX	17.00 C	17.15	18.04
SO	17.10	17.25	18.05
SX	17.25 B	17.40	18.27
SX	17.30 C	17.45	18.35
SO	17.40	17.55	18.47
SX	17.55 B	18.10	18.57
SX	18.00 C	18.15	19.04
SO	18.10	18.25	19.05
	18.40 C	18.55	19.47

then at the following
minutes past each hour

	10 C	25	05
	40 C	55	47

until

	21.10 E	21.25	22.05
	21.40	21.55	22.51

4 A memory problem

Have you got a good memory? All these things happened in the 1960s — one in each year from 1960 to 1969. Can you put them in the right order?

Neil Armstrong landed on the moon
Princess Margaret got married
The Russians entered Prague
First James Bond film released
President Kennedy was assassinated
England won the soccer World Cup
Sir Winston Churchill died
The first heart transplant took place (where?)
Luther King won the Nobel Peace Prize
The Berlin Wall was built

(Obviously you can also do the 1970s; get students to check their answers by going to the library etc., and perhaps use events better known in their country etc.)

5 Is it true?

Are the following statements true or false?

(a) Bordeaux used to be the capital of France.
(b) Konrad Adenaur was 90 when he died.
(c) Spain and Portugal used to be ruled by the same king.
(d) The king of Sweden married a Belgian who became his queen.
(e) Amsterdam is the capital of Holland.
(f) No Spanish team has ever won the European cup.
(g) Luxembourg is the smallest country in Europe.
(h) Cologne Cathedral is the largest church in Europe.

(Obviously these sentences are only examples. You should use a set of say half-a-dozen about the pupils' own country, history, etc. Remember, the purpose of these is to make them discuss in groups, so you should choose items that they are *unlikely* to be sure about.)

6 Other situations

Give one student a tourist brochure; others ask when things are open, how much they cost and so on.

One student has a timetable, the others ask questions.

A group of students has three or four advertisements for similar things — holidays, places to stay, things to do etc — and discuss which they prefer. Students have information about using the telephone — leaflet or poster — and look for answers to specific questions and/or discuss the best course of action.

Remember that when you use authentic material it may be objected that it can only be used by pupils whose English is good enough for them to 'understand' it. This is not true. Anyone in England who wants to understand a train timetable or advertisement needs to do so regardless of the level of their grasp of the language. The important thing is to handle the material in different ways; for less advanced students it's enough if they can get the *gist* of what they want and the answers to a few specific questions (Is it open on Sundays? When is the last train?) Don't forget, these materials will be difficult to get hold of when you are abroad so, as we said in chapter 6, you should look for some before you go.

4.2 Appropriacy exercises

Very often students know a lot of English and can produce formally acceptable language. In other words, it doesn't contain grammatical mistakes. At the same time, it most definitely does not seem natural and may convey an idea of disinterest or surliness which they do not intend. The following activities are to encourage pupils to be more sensitive to using language which it not only structurally accurate, but appropriate too.

THE DIALOGUE EXERCISE

A dialogue is presented to the class (either in writing, on tape, or by you reading it aloud). This is followed with questions about the language. In all cases, when pupils answer the questions you should ask them *why* they think that and what particular items in the dialogue lead them to think so. Obviously the dialogue should contain specific phrases that are formal, friendly, old-fashioned, trendy, or whatever.

Dialogue 1
A: You've just been to Tenerife, haven't you?
B: Yes.
A: Did you have a good time?
B: Not really, no.
A: I'm sorry to hear that. What went wrong?
B: The weather was pretty awful.
A: Really?
B: Yes, it was disappointing.
A: That's a bit surprising at this time of year, isn't it?
B: I suppose so.
A: What was the hotel like?
B: Oh it was all right.
A: And did you have good food?
B: Well I thought it was all right, but Jill wasn't very keen.

A: Not used to it I suppose?
B: That was probably it. She was a bit off colour anyway.
A: Oh, nothing too serious I hope.
B: No, it was nothing much. She's always complaining you know.

Here are some questions:

Do the two people know each other well?
Are they *close* friends?
Is either of them annoyed?
How do you know?
What sort of holiday did B have?
What was the food at the hotel like?
What was wrong with Jill?
Who do you think Jill is?

(Other questions should suggest themselves: notice in some cases students are interpreting particular items (off colour), in some cases the style (B answering with so many very short answers), in some cases extensively (B seems a bit sour altogether). It's most apparent if you contrast it with the next dialogue).

Dialogue 2
A: Hello, I haven't seen you for a while.
B: No, we're just back from Tenerife actually.
A: Oh, how lovely.
B: Well, actually, I'm afraid it wasn't. I got a bit of a tummy bug, most unpleasant.
A: Oh how frightful. All right now?
B: Well, picking up you know, but still a bit dicky.
A: Well, you'd better take it easy. That sort of thing can take a lot out of you, you know. What sort of weather did you have?
B: Absolutely diabolical – sun hardly shone at all.
A: Oh how terribly unfortunate. You *have* been unlucky, haven't you.
B: I beg your pardon?
A: I was just saying how unlucky you'd been.
B: You're too right. I think we both wished we'd stayed at home.

Here are two simpler ones:

Dialogue 3 (on a train)

A: Is this taken?

B: No, you're all right. Would you like me to move my bag?

A: No, it's all right dear, I can manage.

B: It's rather crowded, isn't it.

A: Well Fridays is usually like this.

B: Really, I don't use the trains much myself.

A: You're lucky love, I do this twice a day.

Dialogue 4

A: You did remember to post that letter for me, didn't you.

B: Oh hell, no, it completely slipped my mind.

A: Oh.

B: What's the matter?

A: It doesn't matter.

B: I'll drop it in at the post office for you on my way home.

A: It's all right. I'll take them out in a few minutes myself.

B: No, no, no, I'll go. It's no trouble. I'm sorry I forgot earlier.

A: I *said* it didn't matter. I'll take them myself as soon as I've finished what I'm doing.

B: OK please yourself, but I could just as easily drop them in about half-past five.

A: I think I'd rather know they've *definitely* gone.

B: You're probably right. It *is* probably best if you do it yourself.

WHO'S SPEAKING? EXERCISES

A number of similar expressions are listed together with a number of people. Pupils pair up the expressions and the speakers appropriately.

This exercise can be made slightly more difficult by giving only the list of expressions and asking pupils themselves to provide appropriate speakers.

One of the important distinctions you can make for them here is the sort of expression which is only used by a functionary — a person performing a service. So, for example, a hotel receptionist will say, 'What name is it please?' — whereas this would sound very odd if you asked somebody at a party the same question.

Who's speaking

Look at the expressions in column 1. Can you pair them up with the speakers in column 2?

Column 1

1 What's your name?
   What name is it please?
   I'm afraid I didn't catch your name.
   Who's calling please?
   I'm afraid I don't know your name.

2 It's a great pleasure to meet you.
   Hi there.
   How do you do.
   Hello.
   Good morning.

3 Close the door, would you.
   Would you mind closing the door please
   Would you close the door, please.
   Can you close the door, please.

4 Sorry sir, there's no smoking in here.
   Excuse me, I'm afraid smoking isn't allowed in here.
   Haven't you seen the sign?
   Oh, you're not going to smoke, are you?

5 Give us a hand.
   Do you mind giving me a hand with this, please.
   Could you PLEASE help me.
   Would you help me with this, please.

Column 2

1 A person speaking on the phone
   A hotel receptionist
   A person at a party
   A teacher
   Someone who has already told you his name

2 Your brother
   Your bank manager
   Someone you are introduced to
   A visitor in your office
   A very important person

3 A stranger
   A colleague
   A good friend
   Your wife/husband, etc

4 A very good friend
    A rude stranger
    A polite stranger
    The ticket collector
5 Someone you're annoyed with
    A colleague
    A good friend
    A stranger

Who said it?

1 (a)   Can I open the window please?
   (b)   Could I open the window please?
   (c)   Would you mind if I opened the window please?
   (d)   I think I'll open the window if you don't mind.
   (e)   Goodness, it's so hot in here isn't it.
2 (a)   Bottoms up!
   (b)   Your very good health.
   (c)   Cheers.
   (d)   Round the teeth, round the gums, look out stomach here it comes.
3 (a)   I'm not sure I follow you.
   (b)   What the hell do you mean by that?
   (c)   Sorry, I'm not with you.
   (d)   I'm afraid I don't understand.
   (e)   I'm afraid I don't see what you're getting at.
4 (a)   You're wrong.
   (b)   Are you quite sure?
   (c)   I think you're mistaken there, actually.
   (d)   That just isn't true.
5 (a)   Do you think you could possibly move your bag please?
   (b)   Would you mind moving your bag?
   (c)   Would you mind moving your bag, please?
   (d)   Oh come on now, get your bags out of the way.
6 (a)   I'm so sorry to hear that.
   (b)   What a pity.
   (c)   Tough luck!
   (d)   Hard cheese!
7 (a)   No.
   (b)   No, I haven't.
   (c)   No, I'm afraid I haven't.
   (d)   No, I most certainly have NOT.

HOW DO THEY FEEL?

A series of expressions are given — preferably in a short context (three or four lines is enough) — and pupils try to say whether the expressions show anger, annoyance, sympathy, enthusiasm or whatever.

If these expressions are given to the pupils out of context they are usually too difficult.

How do they feel?
Here are some expressions that are suitable to use in *how do you feel* exercises. If you want to use them you should put each in a short context. Remember, these are almost impossibly difficult out of context.

1   What on earth do you think you're doing?
2   What the hell do you think you're playing at?
3   What do you think YOU'RE playing at?
4   Who do you think I am?
5   You WOULD think that, wouldn't you.
6   If you like.
7   Certainly not.
8   You don't say!
9   I really would like to, but I'm afraid I just can't make it.
10 Do you think I'm made of money?
11 Well, it was rather *silly* of you.
12 I follow you but I'm not sure I agree with you.
13 I'd rather not talk about it if you don't mind.
14 Oh that *is* a pity.
15 I don't really think it was necessary.
    I really think that was unnecessary.
    I really think that was totally unnecessary.
    Do you really think that was necessary?
16 Come on, it can't be as bad as it seems.

APPROPRIACY TEST – POSSIBLE OR IMPOSSIBLE

Pupils are presented with a series of two-line dialogues (either written or read aloud). Each question consists of an opening line and four responses. The pupils mark each of the responses *possible* or *impossible*.

Possible means this would be a normal, neutral, friendly thing to say to an acquaintance (not a close friend).

The number of *possible* responses given for the different questions should vary so that none, one, two, three or all four may be correct.

Very often, for example, pupils confuse *excuse me* and *sorry*. Although they may produce the correct item on a particular occasion there is a good chance that they will produce the alternative (incorrect) item on another occasion. By presenting them with a range of answers and finding which they think are possible, one is able to correct these mistakes before they become ingrained.

It is important when doing such a test to explain to the pupils that you are looking for a natural, friendly answer to an acquaintance, not just something which is structurally correct. For example, native English speakers (when speaking to strangers /acquaintances) would not produce any of answers ii), iii) or iv) in this example:

A: It's a lovely morning isn't it.
B: (i) Yes it is, isn't it.
    (ii) Yes.
    (iii) Yes it is.
    (iv) Do you think so. I think it's a bit cold.

These tests can surprise the pupils a lot and stimulate a great deal of interest and discussion because they are surprised. It's usually true to say that most pupils make a lot more mistakes than they expect and, rather than being depressed by this, they find it stimulating and amusing. It is also worth knowing that very often younger pupils are as good (or as bad) at this sort of test as older ones, and frequently teachers are as bad (or good) as their pupils.

If you are going to construct such a test, you will find it difficult to do so on your own. It is much easier if you work together with two or three other native speakers.

Appropriacy test

Look at these two-line dialogues. In each case mark each reply *P* if you think it is a possible reply. If you think it is impossible mark it *I*. There may be one, two, three or four possible answers, or they may all be impossible.

A possible answer is something you could say to a stranger or an acquaintance – someone you do not know very well.

1 A: Hello John how are you.
    B: (a) Thank you, very well.
        (b) Fine thanks and you?
        (c) Very fine thanks. And you?
        (d) Not very well.

2 A: Excuse me, do you mind if I open the window?
    B: (a) No, please do.
        (b) No that's all right.
        (c) Yes please.
        (d) No I don't mind.

3 A: John sends his regards.
    B: (a) Oh.
        (b) Send them back.
        (c) If you see him give him *my* regards.
        (d) Thank you very much.

4 A: Do you mind if I open this window?
    B: (a) No.
        (b) I'd rather you didn't.
        (c) Please don't.
        (d) I don't want you to, please.

5 A: Excuse me, could you tell me the time please.
    B: (a) No I can't.
        (b) No it isn't possible.
        (c) I'm sorry I'm afraid I can't.
        (d) I'm afraid I haven't got my watch on.

6 A: I'm so sorry I'm late.
    B: (a) Oh, that's quite all right.
        (b) It doesn't matter.
        (c) I see.
        (d) Oh, don't worry. It's all right.

7 A: Please have some more.
    B: (a) No.
        (b) No thank you.
        (c) I'm sorry but I just couldn't manage any more.

  (d) No thank you I've had enough of
      it.

8 A: Would you mind opening the window
       please.
   B: (a) Certainly.
       (b) Yes.
       (c) It's my pleasure.
       (d) Not at all.

9 A: I'm just back from Italy.
   B: (a) I see.
       (b) Are you?
       (c) How interesting.
       (d) Italy?

10 *On the phone.*
    A: Hello, could I speak to Jane please.
    B: (a) This is her.
        (b) It's me.
        (c) You're speaking to her.
        (d) Speaking.

11 *In the cafe.*
    A: Yes?
    B: (a) Could I have a cup of tea please.
        (b) Please could I have a cup of tea.
        (c) Could I please have a cup of tea.
        (d) Tea please.

12 *On a train.*
    A: Terrible day, isn't it.
    B: (a) Yes awful, isn't it.
        (b) Do you really think so?
        (c) Yes it is.
        (d) It is, isn't it.

13 A: Have you heard, I've failed my
        driving test again.
    B: (a) I'm sorry.
        (b) Oh, I am sorry.
        (c) That's a pity.
        (d) Please accept my condolences.

14 A: I thought you'd like a ticket so I got
        one for you.
    B: (a) Thank you.
        (b) That's good.
        (c) Oh, thank you very much, that
            was kind of you.
        (d) I'm pleased because I hadn't seen
            it.

15 A: Excuse me, could you tell me the way
        to the station please?

    B: (a) I don't know.
        (b) I'm a stranger, you'll have to ask
            someone else.
        (c) I'm afraid I'm a stranger here
            myself.
        (d) No idea, perhaps that policeman
            could help you.

INFORMATION-ONLY DIALOGUES

We have already discussed these in section 4.1.
However, remember they are also useful in
pointing out to pupils that it is inappropriate
just to 'answer' in a conversation. You are
expected to contribute and develop the
conversation, so those dialogues have a use here
too.

REARRANGED DIALOGUES

Particularly for younger pupils, one of the
easiest ways to introduce the idea that a
conversation is not just a series of questions
and answers is to give them (on an overhead
transparency or on the blackboard) the mixed-
up lines of a natural dialogue (it should literally
be a dialogue – between no more than two
people). All pupils have to do is to rearrange
the lines to make a natural dialogue.

The dialogue you use should have most of the
lines structurally linked:

It's a lovely day, *isn't it?*
Yes, *it is,* isn't it? But it was very cold
    yesterday, *wasn't it?*
Yes, *it was.* I *went* to London.
Oh, *did* you.

The whole thing can be made much more
difficult by including some of the following one
word lines:

Really?
Please.
Sorry?

Other very short responses (*I'm afraid not. Not
really*) also make it difficult.

You could put younger children in teams and
see who can rearrange the dialogue most
quickly. Although this activity may look rather

trivial, you are in fact forcing pupils to concentrate on the linguistic links which make conversation something more than the information-only type of dialogue.

The object of these practices is to make pupils aware of the fact that what one speaker says is linked to what the previous speaker has said. These practices are in increasing order of difficulty.

Remember how important it is not to answer just *yes* or *no* on its own. A normal friendly reply is much longer. Link up the answers in column 2 with the questions in column 1.

Column 1
1 Was it late?
2 Did they get there on time?
3 Was he angry?
4 Did he appreciate it?
5 Did she like it?
6 Is it on tonight?
7 Are they disappointed?
8 Do you have to wear a tie?
9 Does it cost a lot?
10 Does she work here?

Column 2
A: Yes, it does as a matter of fact.
B: Yes, he was as a matter of fact.
C: Yes, she does, only part time, though.
D: Yes, it was actually.
E: Yes, you do I'm afraid.
F: Yes, she did actually.
G: Yes, they did actually.
H: Yes, they are a bit.
I: Yes, it is as a matter of fact.
J: Yes, he did as a matter of fact.

Dialogue 1
1 Did you. How's she?
2 Didn't you?
3 Yes it is, isn't it. I've just been shopping.
4 Hello, it's a lovely day, isn't it.
5 Did she! No, I didn't know.
6 Have you. Did you buy much?

7 Oh, very well. You know she had a baby last month.
8 No, not much really. But I met Jane.

Dialogue 2
1 Oh, I don't really know. Are you going out?
2 Are you? I didn't know you two knew each other.
3 What are you doing this evening?
4 Yes, I am actually. I'm going out with Mary.
5 Didn't you! Oh, yes, we've been seeing a lot of each other recently.
6 Have you! Did you meet at work?
7 Was it really! He didn't tell me he had a party.
8 No we didn't as a matter of fact. It was at John's.

Dialogue 3
1 Can you! That's interesting.
2 Wouldn't you? I'd go again.
3 Yes, you are, aren't you . . . unfortunately.
4 I've just been to Majorca.
5 No, you wouldn't, would you. I can understand that.
6 Have you. I'd never go there.
7 Yes it is, isn't it. I'm beginning to understand you.
8 Would you? I wouldn't go once, never mind twice!

Dialogue 4
1 That's right, the one when Bob got married.
2 Really? It's not often that happens, is it.
3 I can't remember what, but I do remember when.
4 Yes, I remember that.
5 Oh yes, it was at that party.
6 John and I couldn't agree, I'm afraid.
7 No, the last time was about two years ago.
8 Do you? What was it about?

Dialogue 5
1 You sound surprised.
2 As well as can be expected, thanks.
3 Shocking day isn't it?
4 Are you really?

5 Really. And you had bad weather there.
6 Majorca.
7 Not too bad thanks. Are you keeping well?
8 We did.
9 I am a bit. I thought you liked comfort.
10 Did you? How disappointing. Where did you go?
11 We are going camping this year.
12 We do. Don't worry, it's a very modern caravan.
13 Isn't it awful, we've just come back from our holiday and we had awful weather all the time.
14 Hello, how are you?

Dialogue 6
The first and last lines of this dialogue are in the correct place. The others need to be rearranged.
1 Hello.
2 Yes, I'm afraid so.
3 Not too bad thanks. Chilly this morning, isn't it.
4 Oh, much better thanks.
5 Oh, don't worry it could have been much worse.
6 Awful, isn't it. John was telling me the other day you'd hurt yourself.
7 Well, I've been a bit off colour myself recently actually.
8 What on earth did you do?
9 Really, what a dreadful nuisance.
10 Fine, thanks, and you?
11 Really, nothing serious I hope.
12 How are you feeling now?
13 Oh, it was nothing serious, I just twisted my ankle.
14 Hello, how are you?
15 Oh no, it's this bug that's been about you know. I feel better now. I think I'll survive.

4.3 Talking about grammar

We have been surprised by the success of getting the pupils to discuss grammar rather than just presenting them with a rule from the teacher or the book. If they can be encouraged to say what they think the explanation is, and how it compares or contrasts with their own language, it is much easier to guide them towards a clearer understanding than they get from an explanation in which they have not been involved. From your point of view, you will find discussing the grammar with them easier than giving rules and, providing you conduct the class in English (we repeat that again), the activity is doubly useful: firstly, pupils are studying the grammar, and secondly they are practising the language of discussion while talking to you. Many teachers become very frustrated when they try to run traditional conversation classes with topic-based discussions. By all means try those but, surprisingly perhaps, you may well find pupils more willing to discuss the language itself, particularly if you encourage them to talk about their own language too. It's one subject that everybody believes he is an expert on!

There are at least three tactics for encouraging this sort of activity:

THE CLOZE TEST

We've already discussed cloze dialogues. Here you take a text and delete from it important structural words – auxiliary verbs, irregular past tense forms, etc. and ask pupils to fill in possible words. Again, you should vary the words you delete. Some should have only one possible answer (he could have . . . asked) others should allow restricted choice (he . . . have been asked). Others may have a very wide choice (he could have been . . .).

If pupils produce the correct answer, this serves as a useful revision. If they do not, it reveals gaps in their knowledge which you can either deal with yourself or mention to their class teachers. If you make up a text yourself it is possible to have an amusing or exciting story, and by deleting suitable words you can give the pupils a chance to make the story even more amusing!

If you have older pupils and you want to try this exercise you should delete extensively; that is to say, you should cross out words near the beginning that are uniquely determined by something which comes near the end. The pupil thinks he has a free choice at the beginning but must bear in mind that when he reads the rest of the text he may need to go back and change what he has already done. An example should make this clear. The text begins, *The . . . curled up on the rug at his master's feet.* There appears to be a free choice between, for example, *dog* and *cat.* If towards the end of the text *it* purrs, all those who have chosen *dog* will have to go back and correct themselves. It can be frustrating but fun for the pupils to discover that the murdered man was shot after they've given the criminal a knife in the first line!

CLOZE TESTS

Can you fill in one word in each space in the following. Sometimes there is only one correct word but at others you have a choice of words.

By the end of the twenty-first . . . there . . . well be people living in . . . who . . . never visited Earth, but . . . that they can . . . in touch with . . . families, . . . they happen to be . . . Earth, the moon, or . . . else in the system, . . . will all . . . wearing a wristband. Through this, . . . a . . . orbiting computer, . . . will be able to talk to any . . . person in the solar system, . . . by speaking that person's computer number . . . their wristband . . . . . . their wristbands can be . . . . . . the million at a cost of only about £15 each. . . . is difficult to . . . that it is . . . more . . . twenty years . . . the first satellite was . . . .

The haunted house

. . . house is haunted. It . . . been for . . . two years now. Well . . ., the house isn't haunted but the garage . . . . I'm not . . . about it, . . . I know the ghost is friendly. I . . . hear him laughing. That's the . . . annoying thing, because he has a very . . . laugh and you . . . hear it all . . . the house. I've . . . seen him but I'd like to. I don't know . . . who has met . . . . All . . . friends think it would be . . . to meet this . . . . . . I said, the first time I . . . he was . . . was two years . . . . . . the middle . . . the

night, with no warning at all, I . . . this loud laugh.

(Notice that the easiest way to make these up is to use texts from ordinary textbooks. The most difficult are not usually when you delete difficult words but rather when you delete structural words – *as, though, than* and so on.)

SPOT THE DIFFERENCE

Students are presented with pairs (or small groups) of sentences which are similar in meaning. They try to explain the difference. The differences may involve grammar, connotational meaning, register, or on occasions simply be two sentences that look similar but have quite different meanings.

(a) Grammatical explanations

1 The car stopped when the lights changed.
   The car was stopping when the lights changed.
2 They live in Dortmund.
   They're living in Dortmund.
3 I've already waited for half-an-hour.
   I've already been waiting for half-an-hour.
4 I watched the television until 10 o'clock.
   I was watching the television until 10 o'clock.
5 He lived in Florence.
   He used to live in Florence.
6 I'm leaving tomorrow.
   I'll leave tomorrow.
   I'm going to leave tomorrow.
   I leave tomorrow.
   I'll be leaving tomorrow.
7 I'll be annoyed if he doesn't come.
   I'd be annoyed if he didn't come.
8 I used to live in that part of the town.
   I'm used to living in that part of the town.
9 I didn't see him, did you?
   I haven't seen him, have you?
10 I like to go to the theatre.
   I'd like to go to the theatre.
11 I have lunch at work.
   I'm having lunch at work.
12 I always meet her at the station.

I'm always meeting her at the station.

13 You mustn't do that.
You needn't do that.

14 Would you like a cake?
Would you like some cake?

15 Someone in the office will be able to help you.
Anyone in the office will be able to help you.

16 There are too many shadows in this photograph.
There's too much shadow in this photograph.

17 What are you doing?
What do you do?

18 Is there time to catch the train?
Is it time to catch the train?

(b) Differences of register

All the sentences are correct. Can you say in which situation each sentence is appropriate?

19 Excuse me, is this seat taken?
Excuse me sir, is this seat taken?

20 Hang on a minute, I'll see if he's in.
Could you hold on for a moment please, I'll see if he's available.

21 Pass the salt.
Pass the salt, would you.
Would you pass the salt, please.
Excuse me, I wonder if you could pass the salt please.

22 Can I open the window?
Would you mind if I opened the window?

23 Would you like some tea?
Do you want some tea?
Do you like tea?

(c) Various examples

24 He stopped to smoke.
He stopped smoking.

25 I'm rather sure he'll want to come.
I'm fairly sure he'll want to come.

26 He's worked hard recently.
He's hardly worked recently.

27 Do you remember doing it?
Did you remember to do it?

28 She's a pretty small girl.
She's a pretty little girl.

MAKING OPPOSITES

Very often if we wish to express two opposite meanings, we require two sentences which are quite different in form. Only rarely is one the direct structural negative of the other (incidentally, this shows very clearly why so many students who are good at English at school still have a lot of trouble speaking fluently and naturally. Most teaching is still structural and, as we've already said, one of your main functions should be to encourage pupils to be able to use the language in more than a purely structural way).

A group of sentences is given to the pupils and they are asked to provide the opposites. Again, because these are not obvious and pupils will make a lot of mistakes, they usually find them frustrating at first but ultimately fascinating and fun. They work best if you are not too helpful initially, so that when pupils give wrong answers you just say (with a smile) 'No, that's wrong, try again'.

Making opposites

Sometimes making opposites is easy:

I can swim   I can't swim
But sometimes the opposite is quite different:
Would you like some more tea?
Yes, please   No, thank you.

Can you say what *B* should say to give the opposite meaning in these cases:

1 A: Would you like to come to a party on Saturday?
  B: Oh yes, thank you, I'd love to.

2 A: Excuse me, do you know where the station is please?
  B: Certainly, it's just down there on the right.

3 A: Do you mind if I open the window?
  B: No, not at all, please do.

4 A: You don't mind if I bring a couple of friends with me, do you.
  B: No, of course not, that'd be really nice.

5 A: You've met John before, haven't you.

   B: Yes, we've met. Hello again.

6 A: Could you change a pound, please?

   B: With pleasure, just a moment please.

7 A: You can speak French, can't you.

   B: Yes, I learned at school.

8 A: What time do you make it please?

   B: It's about twenty-past three.

9 A: You've got the tickets, haven't you.

   B: Yes, they're in my pocket.

10 A: I suppose you'll be there on Saturday.

   B: Yes, of course.

4.4 Practising lexical items

With younger pupils you may well want to revise or extend their vocabularies. With older pupils you will want to give them some words and expressions which are not in their textbooks or which are a feature of colloquial spoken English. Remember that you will often want to teach older pupils expressions as lexical items (in other words without explaining their constituent parts, treating the whole phrase as a single item). Learning vocabulary and lexis, which is not the most exciting of language learning activities, can of course be improved by doing it in the form of games or competitions.

Here are some single sentences where making the opposite can be tricky.

1 I think she must be foreign.

2 Hang on a moment, I'll only be a minute.

3 You must be there by 9 o'clock.

4 I'll tell him as soon as I see him.

5 Young people have more opportunity than they had twenty years ago.

6 You don't need as much sleep as you get older.

7 This is impossible – I'm never going to understand it.

8 If you put *not* in a sentence it usually makes the meaning negative.

(Needless to say, some of these are not intended to be taken too seriously!)

ELIMINATION PROBLEMS

Pupils are given a list of (an odd number of) words and a series of clues. Each clue takes two words from the list. After solving all the clues the 'odd' word is left.

The pairs can obviously be pairs of synonyms, pairs of opposites, two words that make a phrase (letter box, time table) or words that are associated with each other. If you make up such puzzles you should use a preponderance of words which you are sure the pupils already know. Then add a few that are on the edge of their vocabularies.

Cross it out – 1

1	dog	8	green	15	supper
2	boat	9	horse	16	orange
3	blue	10	woman	17	jacket
4	child	11	spoon	18	trousers
5	lamp	12	chair	19	breakfast
6	knife	13	apple	20	telephone
7	plane	14	letter	21	magazine

Clues

(a) two animals

(b) two colours

(c) two fruits

(d) two people

(e) two things to travel on

(f) two things to read

(g) two meals

(h) two things to wear

(i) two pieces of furniture

(j) two things you will find on the table at dinner time

Cross it out — 2

1	box	8	letter	15	bottle
2	lift	9	aerial	16	wireless
3	post	10	record	17	television
4	time	11	driving	18	cassette
5	cards	12	boring	19	directory
6	radio	13	elevator	20	interesting
7	table	14	licence	21	telephone

Clues

(a) Two musical players
(b) A book of numbers
(c) You can check when the train leaves in it
(d) You send a lot when you're on holiday
(e) The answers to (d) arrive through this

(f) Two words, one British one American, for the same thing
(g) Two words, one modern one old-fashioned, for the same thing
(h) You might see it on a chimney
(i) You must have one before you use a car
(j) Two opposites

Cross it out — 3

1	fir	8	sole	15	foreign
2	fur	9	soul	16	salmon
3	box	10	near	17	whale
4	cow	11	bear	18	plaice
5	now	12	mean	19	sound
6	male	13	lamb	20	reliable
7	mail	14	beech	21	generous

Clues

(a) Two opposites
(b) They mean the same
(c) They rhyme
(d) An American looks for his post here
(e) They sound the same

(f) Two fish
(g) There is a silent letter in each
(h) Two animals
(i) They begin with the same letter
(j) Two trees

PAIRING PUZZLES

Rather easier than the elimination puzzles are those when pupils are given two lists, each containing an equal number of items, and have to pair up the corresponding words or expressions.

This can obviously be done with synonyms, words of opposite meaning, expressions where one column contains colloquial expressions and the other the 'straight' synonym, or words which are associated.

Puzzle 1

Make pairs of opposites using one word from list 1 and one word from list 2.

List 1	List 2
heavy	polite
easy	plump
special	bent
straight	difficult
enormous	dull
slim	light
funny	ugly
sharp	ordinary
gorgeous	tiny
rude	blunt

Puzzle 2

Make pairs of opposites, using one word from list 1 and one word from list 2.

List 1	List 2
tall	slow
fat	interesting
fast	open
dark	light
dull	thin
closed	narrow
easy	unpleasant
nice	difficult
weak	short
broad	strong

Puzzle 3

Look at the following list of words. There are 13 pairs of opposites and one odd man out. Can you give the opposite of the odd word?

1	poor	10	serious	19	cowardly
2	slim	11	plump	20	doubtful
3	cruel	12	minute	21	silent
4	rigid	13	enormous	22	wealthy
5	noisy	14	flexible	23	disastrous
6	certain	15	sensible	24	courageous
7	scarce	16	ignorant	25	successful
8	coarse	17	abundant	26	well-informed
9	smooth	18	humorous	27	pig-headed

Puzzle 4

Look at the expressions in column 1. Can you make the correct pairs with the explanations in column 2? All the expressions are to do with the weather.

Column 1	Column 2
1 It's drizzling	(a) It's very hot
2 It's rather muggy	(b) It's very cloudy
3 It's clouding over	(c) It's a bit foggy
4 It's sweltering	(d) It's raining – but only a little
5 It's pouring	(e) It's raining a lot
6 It's misty	(f) It's hot and sticky
7 It's overcast	(g) The weather's getting better
8 It's clearing up	(h) The weather's getting worse

Puzzle 5

Cross out 13 pairs of opposites from the following list, then give the opposite of the odd man out yourself.

1	loud	10	urban	19	complex
2	rude	11	direct	20	ordinary
3	slim	12	polite	21	cramped
4	matt	13	simple	22	doubtful
5	quiet	14	lenient	23	aggressive
6	rural	15	precise	24	spacious
7	stout	16	certain	25	approximate
8	strict	17	unusual	26	conventional
9	shiny	18	radical	27	roundabout

COLLOQUIAL EXPRESSIONS AND IDIOMS

Foreign teachers often think that their pupils should be taught idioms (*it's raining cats and dogs*). In fact, they will probably sound very odd if they use expressions like that. You must beware too of trying to explain these idioms. (Why not *it's raining dogs and cats*? The answer of course is that this is a lexical item and the question is as silly as asking why a table is called a table. In some cases there are historical reasons why particular expressions have come into the language, but trying to explain them now is often impossible and always fruitless.)

Much more useful to the pupils, often more fun to teach and the sort of thing pupils like to know, are colloquial expressions – things that native speakers use naturally in everyday spoken English but which rarely get into foreign textbooks. It's not worth doing whole lessons on these but it is always useful to have two or three up your sleeve for five minutes at the end of a lesson, or if you want a light-hearted break after some more serious activity. There are basically three ways of doing them:

1 Give the pupils the expression (write it on the board or say it) and ask, 'What do you think this means?' You will be amused by some of their more comical suggestions, but you can of course encourage these – they make this a more light-hearted activity.

2 Give them the expression with one or two words missing (like a cloze sentence) and ask them to supply the missing word(s). For example, write on the board *once in a . . . moon*, then say, 'Here's an expression that means "very rarely indeed". What word is missing?'

3 The most comical (and least pedagogically sound!) is to give the expressions in multiple choice form and ask the class to pick the correct expression. This should only be done occasionally and very light-heartedly since, if you're not careful, it will confuse rather than help them. Here is a single example: *Jack is a bit dull. He can't do anything without help. In fact he's rather a*:

(a) sick swan   *(b) lame duck*
(c) one-legged gull   *(d) dead hen*

You should have no trouble making these up for yourself, and we have given some sample material below. Alternatively, there's a small book which contains 300 examples ready made for you (*Test Yourself on English Idioms* by M. J. Murphy, Hodder and Stoughton, 1968), but remember these are for *fun* with older classes.

Where would you be?
Where would you be if somebody said the following to you:

1 Last orders please.
2 All change! All change!
3 How would you like the money?
4 Rare, medium, well-done?
5 Could I see your boarding card please?
6 Would you take a seat for a moment, please?
7 Going down?
8 Hold tight.
9 Do you want mash with it?
10 Trying to connect you.
11 Do you want to register it?
12 Would you like to try it on?
13 I'm afraid we're out of stock at the moment.
14 Dressing?
15 Brighton's the front four coaches only.
16 How would you like it done?
17 Have you got the odd three please?
18 Same again?

How would you answer?
What would you say to someone who said one of the following to you:

1 Does that ring a bell?
2 What's the catch?
3 Do you get the point?

4 I hope I'm not butting in.
5 Do you mind if we put it up a bit?
6 Nippy, isn't it.
7 Can I square-up with you later?
8 I'm a bit peckish aren't you.
9 Can I top you up?
10 What's the damage?

He's a funny chap
What do these expressions tell you about *he* — perhaps what kind of person he is, what he's just done, how he's dressed, or whatever:
He's
1 on the fiddle
2 on the dole
3 in a huff
4 round the bend
5 in the soup
6 off his rocker
7 a bit uptight
8 up to his eyes
9 scruffy
10 on his last legs
11 really on the ball
12 a bit sheepish
13 a bit browned off
14 completely stumped
15 a bit thin on top
16 a bit long in the tooth
17 in a rut
18 over the moon

How do you feel?
How would you feel if I said:

1 I feel a bit off colour.
2 I've got pins and needles.
3 I was absolutely fuming.
4 I was really fed-up by the time we'd finished dinner.
5 I've just had my jacket pinched.
6 I haven't got a leg to stand on.
7 I feel lousy.
8 He told me to pull my socks up.
9 I had tc put my foot down.
10 My uncle pulled a few strings for me you know.

What makes you say that?
Can you say something — either a single thing or perhaps a short conversation — that would make me say:

1 Come off it.
2 No thanks, I'm just looking.
3 Not up to now.
4 I'm afraid it's not up to me.
5 OK please yourself.
6 I'm not sure, but he must be getting on a bit.
7 I'm sorry, I'm broke.
8 Oh nothing much, how about you.
9 I'm sorry, I just couldn't make it.
10 I'm picking up now thank you.
11 OK, let's put it off then.
12 I don't see how I can get out of it.
13 I'm afraid it was a total write-off.
14 Well, you'd better keep your fingers crossed then.
15 Come on, that was below the belt.
16 I don't think I could face it.
17 I'll give you a buzz then.
18 Touch wood.

Miscellaneous expressions
You may find two or three of these useful as a five-minute filler. Remember, if the pupils use some of these they will sound very odd, so don't teach them – they're strictly for amusement only.

1 He's got his head screwed on.
2 I was pretty chuffed.
3 He does go on a bit doesn't he.
4 Come on, get your finger out.
5 That'll be a doddle.
6 That really gets my back up.
7 He's got her on the brain.
8 You'll just have to grit your teeth.
9 She looks down her nose at people.
10 That's a sight for sore eyes.
11 He can be a bit touchy.
12 He talks through his hat.

4.5 Odd man out exercises

Most of us as children have picked the 'odd man out' from examples like:

apple   pear   banana   potato   peach

This type of puzzle can, however, be exploited in three different ways in the language classroom.

FOR VOCABULARY

In this case the traditional puzzle is suitable. All but one of the words (usually five or six) are linked by meaning. If the pupil understands the words he will be able to identify the odd one.

(a) Vocabulary
To use these in class take a mixed selection and ensure that pupils talk about the answers in English (in groups).
1 Car, lorry, train, caravan, van.
2 Massive, enormous, minute, huge, gigantic.
3 Record, coin, stamp, wheel, ring.
4 Veal, lamb, ham, pork, beef.
5 Bough, bush, leaf, twig, trunk.
6 Bag, case, wallet, briefcase, rucksack.
7 Train, plane, car, taxi, bus.
8 Blink, yawn, wink, squint, stare.
9 Checked, striped, woollen, spotted, plaid.
10 Spanner, saw, screwdriver, pliers, nails.
11 Generous, honest, deceitful, kind, sympathetic.
12 Rush, hurry, gallop, stagger, dash.
13 Shriek, clatter, gabble, mumble, yell.
14 Mare, cow, sow, ewe, dog.

FOR GRAMMAR

The link between the words is grammatical, and of the kind that the foreign student of English is more likely to identify than a native speaker. If you want to construct examples of this kind you should get hold of one of the school grammars used where you are working and look for sections containing groups of words which the pupils learn together.

Such exercises, done in a light-hearted competitive way, can be a useful revision of important work pupils have studied in their main English lessons.

(b) Grammar
1 Got, were, had, are, can.　　　　Got – others auxiliaries.
2 Attractive, light, green, old, black.　　Attractive – not '-er' comparative.
3 Quick, sharp, careful, hard, beautiful.　Hard – others make adverb with -ly.

4	Sheep, child, horse, woman, man.	Horse — only regular plural.
5	Hit, cut, put, let, sit.	Sit — others have principal parts the same.
6	Cost, read, shut, hurt, tell.	Tell — principle parts.
7	Alike, attentive, aloud, asleep, awake.	Attentive — others used only predicatively.
8	Snow, advice, weather, furniture, apple.	Apple — only countable noun.
9	Yours, ours, theirs, hers, my.	My — stands in front of noun.
10	Walk, write, visit, cook, push.	Write — past irregular.
11	Boy, book, house, child, dog.	Child — plural irregular.
12	Content, satisfied, associated, pleased, natural.	Natural — other negatives *dis*.
13	Socks, trousers, scissors, shirts, gloves.	Shirts — others all 'a pair of'.
14	Proper, perfect, polite, popular, personal.	Popular — other negatives *im*.
15	News, women, people, sheep, cattle.	News — always singular.
16	Important, impartial, impertinent, impolite, imperfect.	*Portant* is not a word.
17	Look, glare, gaze, peep, watch.	Watch — others followed by *at*.
18	Historic, economic, electric, politic, dynamic.	*Dynamical* is not a word.
19	Doubt, beauty, intelligence, power, dread.	*Intelligenceful* is not a word.
20	Must, should, have, could, might.	Have — not a modal.

(c) Sound

1	Snowed, played, tried, waited, rained.	Waited — *ed* pronounced /id/.
2	Doubt, bout, bought, drought, out.	Bought — doesn't rhyme.
3	Bow, row, cow, read, tear.	Cow — only one pronunciation.
4	Write, their, mail, case, bough.	Case no alternative spelling for word of same pronunciation.
5	Knee, lamb, finger, palm, knowledge.	Finger — no silent letter.
6	Church, bus, pleasure, dish, praise.	Pleasure — plural adds /z/.
7	Suspect, advise, export, contract, protest.	Advise — others' stress can move.
8	Stationery, principal, table, flower, allowed.	Table — no alternative spelling.
9	Chemistry, inch, Christian, chapel, machine.	Chapel — only one with *ch* pronounced / /.
10	Review, repeat, rejoice, retail, resent.	Retail — pronunciation of *re*.

(d) Miscellaneous

1	Hot, hop, her, hid, hat.	Add *e* at end.
2	Pillar, Christmas, telephone, suitcase, cardboard.	Add *box*.
3	Vile, evil, live, avail, veil.	Four anagrams.
4	Now, tone, pace, flat, trip.	Add *s* at beginning.
5	Pan, man, pit, reed, rat.	Spell backwards.
6	River, weight, knife, clip, news.	Add *paper*.
7	Flavour, theatre, night, colour, plane.	American spellings.
8	Bear, hear, fear, dear, tear.	?
9	Doubt, organise, wonder, spend, write.	?
10	Every, all, each, another, any.	?

TO STIMULATE DISCUSSION

This is by far the most important use of these exercises. The examples should be mixed – some vocabulary, some grammatical, and ideally one or two items should be very very difficult (if you are very brave they should have no real answer at all). They are then presented to the class with something like the following introduction: 'You did some of these the other week and I found another one but I'm afraid I can't do it myself. I can do most of the examples but not no. 6. See if you can do it. Do the others just to get the idea and see if you can do the one I can't do.'

The important thing here is not whether they can do the examples but that if they cannot they should be encouraged to guess, speculate and talk about what the answer can and cannot be. The objective, known only to you, is the language they use to talk about the problem, not the solution itself. In short, this use is one example of a whole range to which we now turn our attention.

4.6 Puzzles to stimulate language

We have already mentioned the use of information gap situations where there is usually a 'gap' between one pupil and the class or between individual pupils. Any sort of puzzle which they try to solve linguistically is similar, except the gap is between the author or compiler and the whole class. If you decide to use these puzzles you should explain to the class that you are concerned with the language they use to solve the puzzle. So, when they get stuck they must not just sit and look at it or revert to their own language. *The objective is that they should discuss, reason and argue in English.* Most good bookshops have a section devoted to puzzle books, often in the children's department. One or two well-chosen books should provide you with a wealth of materials. They are usually particularly easy to find around Christmas time and may well be a source of new ideas for the new term after the Christmas break.

THREE KINDS OF PUZZLE:

Word puzzles – we have already discussed most of the basic types.
Intelligence questions – obviously you choose puzzles/problems at a level which the pupils will find challenging but not beyond them. Remember, the main purpose is to encourage them to discuss and argue about the answers.

1 Three men went out to dinner. The bill was thirty dollars. Each man gave a ten dollar bill to the waiter. He took the bill to the office and they said there'd been a mistake. The bill should have been twenty-five dollars, not thirty. The waiter was supposed to give five dollars back to the men. He realised that five was difficult to divide by three, and the men did not really know how much the bill was anyway. So he kept two dollars himself and gave a dollar back to each man. That means each man had paid nine dollars and the waiter had two dollars, but $3 \times 9 + 2 = 29$, not thirty. Where is the other dollar?

2 A man drove his car one mile to the top of a mountain. His speed was 20 miles an hour. How fast must he drive one mile down the other side so that his average for the whole (two mile) journey is 40 miles an hour?

3 Here are some simple (?) paradoxes:

(a) A frog is at the bottom of a 30-foot well. Each hour he climbs 3 feet and slips back 2. How many hours does it take for him to get out?

(b) The fast train leaves A for B at exactly the same time as the slow train leaves B for A. The fast train travels at 100 miles an hour, the slow train at 60 miles an hour. Which train is further from A when they meet?

(c) Two fathers and two sons leave town, but the population only goes down by three. How is that possible?

(d) A clock strikes six in five seconds. How long does it take to strike twelve?

(e) A man is looking at a picture; he says:
Brothers and sisters have I none,
But this man's father is my father's son.
Who is he looking at?

Solve-a-crime

Very popular indeed is the short crime story where the pupil has to identify the criminal and the clues to provide the evidence. There is a book of problems of this kind available in paperback (*Solve-a-Crime* by A. C. Gordon, W. Foulsham and Co.). It is a very cheap book with 60 crimes for pupils to solve. If you use the book you will probably find it best to read the story aloud to the class. In some cases it is wise to go through the story in advance and change a few of the more difficult vocabulary items. Most of the stories, however, are written in simple English and the pupils should have little trouble following. Here is an example of one of the stories (with answer).

The Case of the Body in the Barn

You arrive at the large country home of wealthy Keith Kendall. Terry Ahern and Don Benning, the junior partners in Kendall's firm, lead you to the barn at the rear of the house. Inside, lying face up on the floor, is Kendall's corpse, with a kitchen knife sticking out of his chest.

You dust the handle of the knife and find one set of well-defined fingerprints. Then you take prints of Ahern and Benning, and compare them with the ones on the knife.

'The only prints on the knife are yours, Ahern,' you say. 'But you've told me the knife comes from the kitchen in the house and that you haven't been in the kitchen all day.'

'I can explain,' Ahern replies. 'Don and I drove here today on business. When we couldn't find Mr. Kendall in the house, we started looking for him. The estate is so large, Don and I separated. When I got to the barn, there was Mr. Kendall, with that knife in him! I started to pull the knife out — that's how my fingerprints got on it — and that's just when Don came walking in.'

Don Benning says, 'You can imagine my horror when I walked into the barn and found Terry bent over the body — holding a knife! His face turned pale when he looked up and saw me.'

'It happened as I said!' shouts Ahern. 'I had no reason to —'

'How about that argument you had with him yesterday?' Benning says. 'You told me afterwards that you were fed up with his constant criticism, and you were going to do something drastic about it!'

'I didn't *kill* him,' Ahern mumbles. He turns to you. 'Could it have been suicide.' 'No it wasn't suicide', you say. 'It was murder, and I'm taking one of you with me for questioning!'

Whom do you suspect, and why?

Answer

(a) You suspect Don Benning. (b) The only fingerprints on the knife were Ahern's, which leads you to believe he is innocent, and that someone wiped the handle clean after the murder and before Ahern touched it. (c) If it had been suicide, Kendall's prints would have been on the handle too. And (d) if Ahern had done it, he would not have been so foolish as to wipe the handle clean and then deliberately incriminate himself by putting his prints back on the handle.

© W. Foulsham & Co. Ltd.

4.7 The pupils' mother tongue and translation

We have already said (several times!) we recommend that you do *not* speak the pupils' native tongue during your classes. That does not mean, however, that use cannot be made of it. After all, one of your objectives in being abroad is to improve your knowledge of your target language and the pupils discussing this can often be a great help to you. We therefore suggest here a number of activities where the pupils draw examples from, translate, or discuss *their own* language. These activities will require more preparation on your part and probably co-operation with a native speaker of the pupils' mother tongue — perhaps the other teachers or a group of your friends — but they are of great use to you and worth a little extra effort.

TRANSLATION DIALOGUES

Prepare in advance short (three to eight lines normally) dialogues written in the spoken style of the pupils' native language. Then ask pupils to translate into English. For lower level pupils, use a neutral (stranger to stranger) style. For older pupils, have a more formal or more friendly dialogue in their own language and ask them to get as close as possible in style to that in their English translations.

Notice the dialogues should not be long, eight lines is enough, and should relate to the *natural* use of the *spoken* language.

FALSE FRIEND TRANSLATIONS

Prepare a series of sentences in the pupils' native language containing an item which always causes a problem when they translate — usually because the word in their own language looks and sounds like an English word, but in fact means something different. Prepare a series of 6 to 12 sentences and ask pupils to translate and discuss them in English. (You will very quickly become aware of these 'false friends' after your first few lessons.)

TRANSLATIONS AND COMPARISON WITH MOTHER TONGUE

It is often helpful, both for the pupils and for you, if you ask them to translate into their own language and compare the result, for a number of activities we have already discussed in this chapter. Ask them to translate, and then comment in English on their translations. You do not need to speak their language yourself, though of course it can be helpful sometimes to recognise or guess something they say.

You may well find it helpful to do this with the activities which we discussed in sections 5.1d, 5.1e, 5.1f, 5.2a,b,c, 5.3b,c, 5.4a.

Chapter 5

Some basic techniques for more formal lessons

Sometimes assistants find themselves without much choice about what they should do or how they should do it. They occasionally have to take formal lessons or try their hands at normal language teaching lessons or evening groups.

5.1 Using Questions

1 COMPREHENSION QUESTIONS

These are supposed to test the pupils' understanding of the text, but very often the questions that teachers ask after reading a text hardly check understanding at all. Look at this text and the questions and answers that follow it:

The doodlebing thrang up the hill.

T: Well, now let's have a few questions. What did the doodlebing do?
P1: Thrang up the hill.
T: Good. Where did it thring.
P2: Up the hill.
T: Good. What thrang up the hill?
P3: The doodlebing.
T: Good, yes. And how did it go?
P4: It thrang.
T: Good. Can you give me the principal parts?
P5: Thring, thrang, thrung.
T: Good. Now do you think it was tired when it got to the top?
P: ? ? ?

It should be obvious that only the last question was a comprehension question in the sense that it tested whether the class understood what they had read. The answers to all the other questions can be found in the text. The pupils

who answered those questions either read the answers or made a very simple manipulation. This proved that they knew something about the basic structure of English (what thrang up the hill — the answer will be the first words of the sentence, the subject).

So in asking questions about a text there will be three kinds:

(a) questions where the answer can be read directly from the text (easy)
(b) questions where the answer is a manipulation of the grammar of the text (more difficult)
(c) external questions — you have to understand how the words of the text relate to something outside the text (much more difficult and a real test of understanding).

The easiest way to construct questions is to ask questions that expect the answer no. The question is based on a false assumption. Another short example should show this:

Mr Brown usually gets up at seven o'clock. He has breakfast with his wife and then he goes to work. He usually goes on the bus but this week he's taking his car.

What time does he get up?
The answer can be read
How does he usually go to work?
Again the answer can be read — but note the pupils should say only *on the bus* NOT the full sentence.
Does he usually have breakfast on his own?
A real comprehension question.
Does he always go on the bus?
Another real comprehension question. Notice the answer starts *No . . .*

It is important if you are doing a text or dialogue intensively to ask all three kinds of questions – but remember the first two only practise the language of the text or dialogue and only the third kind tests understanding.

2 QUOTATION QUESTIONS

Very often with a text we do NOT want the pupils to read the answers to questions (type (a) above), but if we are doing a dialogue the opposite is often true. We want the pupils to find the *exact* words which are used to say something in natural English:

A: *Would you like to come to a party on Saturday?*

B: *Oh that'd be marvellous, but I'm afraid I can't. I'm going to see my grandmother.*

T: What does the boy say when he wants to invite his friend to the party?

P1: Do you want to come to a party?

T: No. That's what it *means*, but we don't usually say that. What did he say – what were his exact words?

P2: Would you like to come to a party?

T: That's right . . . Would you like to . . .

Notice these questions have a double purpose. They make sure that the pupils really have found the exact words to make a correct natural English expression, *and* the teacher's first question has also provided an explanation. The explanation here is not what it means, but *why* he said it. If the pupil has provided the words he used when he wanted to invite his friend, clearly he has already understood what the phrase means. It isn't necessary to break it down into its grammatical parts, or to give a long explanation yourself.

If you are doing dialogues it's important to remember that if the pupils are used to texts, they are used to producing the *content* when the teacher asks questions afterwards. When you are asking quotation questions you want the exact language that was used. It may take a while for pupils to get used to this. In the example above we suggest the teacher's

response when the pupil gives the meaning but *not* the exact words.

3 CONVERSATION QUESTIONS

If the pupil has a good teacher, that teacher probably asks a few questions from time to time which appear more personal. (What did you do at the weekend? Did you see . . . on TV last night? Have you been to . . .? Would you like to . . .? Are you interested in . . .?) Very often, however, he asks questions because they practise a structure or phrase which the pupils have just learned (past simple, interested *in*, and so on). For this reason these 'conversations' usually only last two or three lines.

You will probably want to use conversation questions in two different ways:

(1) Interspersed with comprehension questions
The class stay more involved and interested if, when you are doing a text like the one above, you use a sequence of questions like this:

T: What time does Mr Brown usually get up?

P1: Seven o'clock.

T: That's right. What about you?

P1: Er, about 8 o'clock.

T: Oh I see, later than Mr Brown. What about on Saturdays?

P1: Oh, 9 o'clock perhaps.

T: (to another pupil) What about you?

P2: About 9 o'clock as well.

T: But not during the week.

P2: No, about half-past seven.

T: I see, and you?

P3: The same, about half-past seven.

T: Yes, and what about Mr Brown, what does he do then?

This is of course a very simple text and question sequence, but the principle can be used at all levels. Don't separate 'conversation' into a part of the lesson. Make it an integral part of some other activity. A series of short diversions is both more natural and more effective than an attempt at a long conversation session at one time.

(2) Extended conversation

The important thing to remember here is that it is easier to have a conversation if you have something concrete (picture, text or tape) to talk about, and even then it is not easy to start talking about a topic out of the blue. A good idea, then, is to lead pupils into the topic by using a question sequence like this:

(a) Questions which can be answered 'Yes' or 'No'.
(b) Questions which expect short answers. (How often? More than once a month? What else?)
(c) Questions which contain or in them − this is the easiest and most certain way of encouraging pupils away from Yes/No answers. (Do you prefer football or tennis? Have you been to Munich or Frankfurt?)
(d) Concrete questions − ask about the individual, or something that has happened, or that is a question of fact before you go on to (e).
(e) Speculations or judgements. (Someone is talking about what might happen, or shouldn't have happened, or what 'really ought to be done'.) These are linguistically the most difficult and you should work towards them, *not* start with them.

It is often easier to make people say something by saying something yourself which will stimulate a response:

'I really do think the people in this town are funny. I bought a torch at the weekend, but it doesn't seem to work.'

Most experienced teachers will tell you that a conversation class is nearly always more lively and more effective if, instead of asking questions, you say something − preferably about a subject that the pupils know more about than you do and, of course, preferably something just a little contentious!

Perhaps the most effective way of all of making pupils say more is to keep quiet yourself. Once the topic has started don't be afraid to nod or use a gesture of your hand to indicate that you want one of the group to say

something. If you speak they will keep quiet; Very often the most effective form of question is silence.

5.2 Intensive use of a text

DESCRIPTION OF METHOD

(a) Introduce the material
This means two things − give a two or three line summary of the content:

'We're going to look at a text now about the money that's spent on the American space programme. The author talks about how much it costs and whether he thinks it's worth it or not.'

Secondly, presenting to the class *how* you're going to do it:

'Close your books. I want you to listen. I'll read the text. I want you to listen especially for the answers to these two questions. Is the programme getting more or less expensive as time goes on? Does the author think the Americans should spend more or less?'

Or perhaps:

Follow in your books while I read. If there are any words you don't understand or you can't say put a line under them (demonstrate) with your pencil. We'll talk about them after I've read the text.

The idea is to make the pupils active and involved during the first presentation. DON'T let them read (unseen) round the class − they will make lots of mistakes. The reader will understand imperfectly and therefore not interpret the text for the others, there will be a lot of accidental blunders that you feel you have to correct and the whole thing will become muddled.

(b) Pre-questions
Ask some concrete comprehension questions BEFORE the first presentation of the text. This will focus attention and make the situation more natural − usually when we are listening to someone speaking we have a good idea in advance of the sort of things they are likely to

say, though of course we do not know the details.

(c) Presentation of the text

There are different ways of doing this. The least successful is reading unseen round the class.

The alternatives are:

(i) The teacher reads (perhaps only paragraph by paragraph at lower level, longer sections at a higher level).

(ii) The class read after the teacher – sentence by sentence at beginners' level.

(iii) An individual pupil reads after the teacher – sentence by sentence (lower levels) or paragraph by paragraph (at intermediate levels). This is better than unseen reading as the teacher will have already presented a model for some language which would otherwise cause difficulties. The idea is to ensure that the pupil who reads gets it right – it's a presentation of the text not an obstacle course.

(iv) Individual pupils read prepared paragraphs – divide the class into groups (all the people in this line . . . etc). Get different groups to prepare different bits of the text. Go round and help them, ask individual pupils 'is there anything you can't say', 'can you say . . . please' etc. Then, when they have all prepared their own bits get one individual from each group to read the prepared part.

(v) Silent reading. Teachers often forget that if you are reading prominently for content (you're not at the moment interested in them saying all the words of the text) this is the quickest and most natural way of presenting a text.

It need hardly be said that you should not use the same method every time. As with most other things in a classroom, variety usually means improvement, so try to use different methods for different texts.

(d) Check general comprehension (gist)

It's important before trying to use the language of the text to check that the pupils are not completely lost. You must have the experience yourself of reading a difficult text, looking up all the words in the dictionary, understanding all the words and still having no idea what the text was about. In order to check this, you should ask a couple of questions that concentrate not on the detailed language of the text but on the gist of its meaning. If pupils are hopelessly lost at this point, it's wiser to forget the text.

(e) Check comprehension

This means using the sort of question techniques we discussed above. Try to avoid long strings of comprehension questions that only plough through the text. It's usually more effective, more natural and more fun if you intersperse comprehension and conversation questions.

(f) Exploit the text

(i) You could collect together an area of vocabulary and/or do a series of exercises. Texts which have been chosen deliberately as language teaching texts usually suggest a particular exploitation. If you read the text beforehand you soon become aware of, for example, frequent use of the past progressive. It's important to remember that the primary purpose of most language teaching texts is to present particular language, not to stimulate interesting discussion about the content.

(ii) Exploit the content of the text. If students have studied the text and particularly the language in it, they will find it much easier to talk about the content. If you bear this in mind you'll realise that the dichotomy between a formal textbook lesson and a conversation lesson based on some sort of concrete material is not as great as it sometimes appears.

Summary of method
(a) Introduce – content and method.
(b) Pre-questions.
(c) Present – by teacher (or previously prepared pupils).

(d) Check students understand gist.
(e) Check comprehension.
(f) i) Exploit the vocabulary and grammar.
  ii) Exploit the content.

5.3 Extensive use of a text

Texts can be used intensively and extensively or they can be used extensively only. An extensive exploitation will use the text only as a basis for conversation. Here is a summary of the basic method:

1 Introduce the text
2 Give 3 or 4 pre-questions
3 Let students read
4 Explain any problems you anticipate (vocabulary or content)
5 Ask for any further problems
6 Get answers to pre-questions then use comprehension questions to lead into conversation questions and hopefully, to *natural* conversation

5.4 Handling a dialogue

Almost all modern English as a foreign language textbooks have discarded text as the basis for a lesson and replaced it by dialogue. Unfortunately, this practice has not yet spread either to European schools, or, for that matter, to British schools teaching French or German.

In schools and particularly with younger and/or less able pupils, the dialogue has significant advantages over the text. It is usually much shorter, less complex (ie. single extended paragraphs are relatively rare) and from the pupils' point of view more obviously useful. The advantage to the assistant is that he has an up-to-date knowledge of how English is spoken. You may be surprised how difficult it is to say what you would say in a given situation or to comment on *why* something sounds wrong, but one thing is certain, you will almost certainly be better at that than at explaining the grammar of a traditional text lesson!

You may think that dialogue books look too easy. If you're willing to try lessons of this type you will quickly find that although pupils can *understand* everything in a dialogue, when they are required to *reproduce* it, particularly in a situation which is slightly different, their efforts will be very disappointing indeed. This of course means that when you're choosing a dialogue you should never be worried that it will be too easy − if it is, you could always add more language or alternative ways of saying things in the course of the lesson. If, on the other hand, you choose something which is too difficult you'll give yourself considerable problems. The dialogue lesson is based on the fact that the *pupil* is going to perform, not the teacher, so it is important that the material is not beyond him.

In chapter 1 we recommend a number of modern books of dialogues and practice material. Once you know the sort of age range you will be teaching, choose one of these and take it with you. Don't work through the book in traditional fashion but use it rather as a source of ideas for yourself for particular lessons for particular classes. If you pick and choose carefully and modify the dialogues and exercises you'll find that many dialogues can be used over a very wide age and ability range.

The alternative to using textbook dialogues is to write them yourself. Again, this is probably easier than writing texts − they are shorter and can therefore be written on overhead transparency sheets or on a blackboard. If the classrooms have a roller board, then the dialogue can be concealed for part of the lesson and put on show at the appropriate time.

5.5 Writing your own dialogue

(a) Dialogue content should not be limited to pure information about people, places etc. They should contain language which illustrates personality, attitudes, social relationships.

(b) Remember that material in the dialogue should be within the range of experience and interest of your class.

(c) The real purpose of presenting a dialogue is to introduce or provide further practice of language items. For example, working in some of the functional words and phrases on pp. 8–9 is more important than presenting an exciting story.

(d) Keep the dialogue short – eight to ten lines at the most. You can always lengthen them in the class, but the opposite is not true.

5.6   A basic method for teaching a dialogue

(a) Teacher introduces

Usually an anecdote is best: *A friend of mine wanted to ask me to go to Cologne with him at the weekend. What do you think he said to me? Unfortunately, another friend was coming to visit me here so I couldn't go. What do you think I said?* In this way you show that the language the pupils are going to learn is useful in practical situations.

(b) Set a concrete problem

Jack invites Jill to go to . . . on . . . but she can't because . . . Pupils work in small groups (three or four per group) to work out what they will say. This enables pupils with good English to help others with weaker English. Some with more imagination can help even if their English is not so good. Give groups three or four minutes only to prepare answers.

(c) Listen to suggestions and comment on them

Your comments should be leading the pupils towards the language you are going to present. The best comments are in the form of questions: 'What else could he have said there? No that doesn't sound right. What other words will you need to add?' and so on.

(d) Summarise

The teacher summarises and sets several pre-questions to focus attention.

(e) Teacher reads prepared dialogue (pupils cannot see it)

The dialogue is used first as listening comprehension. Read it clearly at about natural speed. It's much easier for the pupils to follow the dialogue if, as you change roles, you change voice slightly (but without ham acting) or change position. Some teachers use their hands as 'puppets' and make their hands talk to each other to show the change of roles. Remember, if you read in a flat, even voice it makes it very difficult to follow.

(f) Teacher checks comprehension

Ask the pre-questions again, then more comprehension questions (aimed at the content) and quotation questions (aimed at the language). Remember that when you ask quotation questions you expect the pupils to reproduce verbatim the appropriate language from the dialogue – it is not enough that they produce something which has the same meaning. You are trying to teach the *specific* language of the dialogue.

(g) Teacher re-reads if necessary

With new pre-questions to help with difficulties that made the second reading necessary.

(h) Pupils see the dialogue for the first time (on stencils, on the overhead projector transparency, or on the blackboard)

The pupils read after the teacher. Obviously different methods of reading are practical here and variety is important – teacher followed by class, phrase by phrase; teacher followed by half classes who answer each other; individual pupils after the teacher.

(i) Pupils work in pairs

By now they should understand the whole dialogue and have said all the important and difficult phrases several times.

(j) Drill(s) to practise selected phrases

It is best to start with very controlled drills – perhaps the pupil has to add a phrase to what he is given:

A Chemist's:
Excuse me, I wonder if you could tell me if there's a chemist's near here please?

Or, slightly more difficult, he may have to change what he said slightly:

Leave early:
Would you mind if I left a bit early, please? (Notice the past form *left*).

It is helpful if the students cannot do the drills completely automatically; in other words they are a small step towards real use of language in a free situation. If you do the following drill you will notice that in examples 3 and 5 you have to make small, but essential changes.

A: I'm going to the cinema tomorrow. Would you like to come with me?

B: I'd love to, but I'm afraid I'm busy tomorrow evening.

Work in pairs. Use this dialogue with the following:
1 I'm going out to the country for the weekend.
2 I'm having lunch with some friends tomorrow.
3 I'm having a party on Friday evening.
4 I'm having a few friends round on Sunday.
5 There are four of us trying to organise a skiing trip at the weekend.
6 We're going sailing on Saturday.

(k) Pupils attempt free situations in pairs/groups

A teacher may either explain these – but this takes quite a long time – or ideally give them out to the pairs/groups on cards. Here is a typical situation to use at the end of an 'invitations' lesson:

Bill asks Richard if he would like to play tennis on Saturday. Richard will be out of town – he's going to visit his sister. Bill suggests the following Saturday. That suits Richard very well.

It's extremely important to remember that, even if you have practised and drilled well up to this point, pupils will still find the free situation extremely difficult and will make lots of mistakes. If you have a full class working together in pairs, all talking at the same time and all making mistakes, it can seem like chaos

but the pupils will usually feel involved and be enjoying the activity. If you have prepared the free situations well, a lot of correct language will be used – and certainly more correct sentences will be said than in a more traditional 'question and answer' based lesson. So don't worry if there are a few minutes of apparent chaos and above all don't cut out this last and most important step. Pupils learn to use language by actually using it – and that means mistakes and a certain amount of noise.

The dialogue-based lesson is much more suitable for the assistant than the traditional text lesson. It is also a useful way of introducing conversation topics which would otherwise fall flat; a lesson on invitations can develop into a chat about games, student parties, and so on. Such a lesson will make a change for the pupils and you will be more confident of your material. If you do it well it will be useful *and* fun.

5.7 Follow-up work

1 Ask them to translate part or all of the dialogue into their own language. For your own interest listen carefully to all the extra words they add. Encourage them to discuss each others' suggestions for translation. It doesn't usually take much to get people to disagree! Encourage them to produce a translation of what they think people *really* say (that's usually the secret to stimulating disagreement). Remember, particularly with older pupils, that they should translate into the same style (register) as the dialogue you have presented. It can be very informative for you if you ask them, 'How would you say that more formally in German? Would that sound natural from two teenagers? Could I say that to your grandmother?' and so on. Get them to talk about their own language, in English, of course.

2 Pick out one of the important words (see pp. 8–9) from the dialogue and ask them to try and produce an equivalent in their own language. Produce more examples in

English, each of which contains this particular word. Get them to translate all of them and see if they always get the same word in their own language. If not, explore the differences together.

3   Try to do the equivalent of *2* the other way round. Collect twenty sentences in their language, each containing the same word. Again, this will work best if you use not a content word, but a word like *bitte, prego, comment* or *s'il vous plaît*. You can either collect the words from the pupils, or collect them in one class and use the examples in another class, or ask the help of a friend or one of the foreign teachers working in the school. (Do not give sentences yourself — it is best not to reveal your knowledge (or ignorance!) of their language).

Ask them to translate the sentences and discuss with them whether the same translation is appropriate each time for the special work. If not, discuss the differences — both in their own language and in English.

Native speakers are extremely sensitive to the use or misuse of these words. They are the words that we use so naturally that they're part of how we behave, and we find people who misuse them odd, confusing or rude, depending on the circumstances. In other words, they are an important part of any language and you will want to be sure that you use the corresponding words in your target language naturally and accurately. Why not let the pupils help you.

Chapter 6

Basic problems of teaching

6.1 General suggestions

It's difficult to give rules for what you should and shouldn't do in a general teaching situation. As soon as you are dealing with a group of people, unpredictable things can happen. We hope the following checklist will give you a framework to help you to prepare yourself for the classes and, if things do go wrong, we hope it will help you to identify the causes of problems.

1 DON'T OVER-REACT

It's all too easy to say or do something as a reaction to what's happening around you and later to regret it. It's very difficult to withdraw what you've said and even more difficult to retreat from a 'position' once you've decided to take a stand. Think first and ask yourself not only what you're going to do now but how you'll handle the reaction to what you do or say. Standing in complete silence for a few seconds is in itself usually enough to make most pupils or classes cool down.

Basically, your objective is very simple, to avoid confrontation. Few pupils are actually 'difficult' but the urge to show off is sometimes strong.

Most 'discipline problems' are very little more than reminding pupils (decisively) that what they did was rather silly or immature but that certainly does not involve confrontation. It's a good guideline that the calmer and quieter you are the more likely you are to handle the class effectively and avoid unpleasantness.

2 DON'T AIM FOR POPULARITY FIRST

The position of the assistant is rather ambiguous − not quite a teacher, certainly not a pupil and, at least from the school's point of view, not really a student either. In many cases, the pupils you are teaching will not be very different in age from yourself and the temptation is very much to aim for success through popularity. Your pupils may not expect you to be a teacher but they will almost certainly expect you to be some sort of leader. If you appear a competent leader − you know what you want and why you want it and are able to ask for it in a clear and pleasant manner − you will become popular because of your competence. Desultory chit-chat once a week will make you unpopular so keep the pupils active.

3 BE EXPLICIT

In general, pupils respond positively to positive direction. If you are indecisive and woolly the pupils will fail to respond, simply because they are not sure what you want. This is particularly important if you *change* what you want.

If people start coming later and later and you think it's time to do something about it, don't jump on people one week if you've tolerated lateness the week before. Say quite clearly that you're not happy about it and that you want people there on time the *next* week.

4 DON'T FORGET THAT THE PUPILS ARE YOUNG

In some cases your pupils will have very limited experience indeed. If they live in large towns or if they have travelled, especially abroad, they may have more to say, but don't expect pupils who live in small towns or in the middle of the country to have opinions and ideas about questions which are probably unfamiliar to them, even if they're eighteen years old. Try to remember what you were like at their age, and how much wider your experience and horizons are now.

5 BE PREPARED

People starting teaching for the first time tend to make two common and opposite mistakes. *(a)* They rely on spontaneity and, with the excuse of 'responding to the pupils' needs' go in unprepared. The most extreme version of this is one which most assistants will recognise − 'Well, what would you like to talk about this morning?' We have tried it ourselves on a number of occasions − nobody has ever wanted to talk about anything! *(b)* They over-prepare; ie write out a list of topics and even a list of particular questions which can be used as a basis for the lesson. Prepare topics and even the questions by all means, but when the prepared notes become the lesson, they become so important that a spontaneous response by the teacher is lost completely and the classes become drab and dull. Contrast your own experience of lecturers who read and those who speak without reading.

Preparation covers a number of things − make sure there is a room available for you and that it is large enough and has sufficient furniture. Find out if there is a blackboard (and chalk!) or any other machinery you may need − perhaps a tape-recorder or overhead projector. If you're going to use a piece of machinery, make sure it works. Put tapes on the machine and find your place *before* the pupils come into the room if at all possible. You will both look and feel rather silly if you have to spin the tape backwards and forwards a dozen times while the pupils sit there waiting.

Remember, too, to prepare yourself. In particular make sure that the way you are dressed is suitable. Try to conform to the general standards of the staff of the school. If you look very different from them you will probably make life more difficult for yourself.

6 ADMIT WHEN YOU DON'T KNOW THINGS

Often the foreign teachers will know a lot more about English from a grammatical point of view than you do. Don't be afraid to admit your ignorance, either to the pupils or to the teachers. You can be sure that if you pretend to know something you'll be found out sooner or later.

7 VARY YOUR LESSONS

Lessons should not always have the same format and, within the lesson, there should be a change of activity and, preferably, a change of pace from time to time. Generally, 60 minutes of the same thing is not as successful as the same 60 minutes would have been if there had been a couple of short activities before, during or after the main activity.

8 KEEP YOUR SENSE OF HUMOUR

A teacher, or anyone in front of a group of people, inevitably does silly or unexpected things from time to time. They're not less funny than they would be if you were sitting in the audience. Remember if you don't laugh *with* the pupils they'll probably laugh *at* you.

9 LET YOUR PERSONALITY SHOW

No-one can respond to someone who behaves like a machine. Try to smile, say what you think yourself, take an interest in what people tell you. Don't forget that the most important thing of all is to come over as a person.

6.2 Language use in the classroom

Most often what teachers are teaching, and how they are teaching it, cannot be confused. The instructions a chemistry teacher gives are in English, but what he is talking about is chemistry. Unfortunately, when you are teaching your own language it's very easy for you and for the pupils to confuse the different reasons that language is used in the classroom.

1 IT'S THE SUBJECT YOU'RE TEACHING

So you give examples, correct pupils, give the correct version of something they have said when they make a mistake, and so on.

2 IT'S THE TEACHING MEDIUM

So, for example, you give instructions in English. In a situation as simple as the following you are using English in ways (i) and (ii):

Pupil   He *buyed* it when he was in England.
You   No, not *buyed, bought.*
Pupil   Yes.
You   No, can you use it please − say the sentence again, but use *bought.*
Pupil   He bought it when he *were* in England.
You   No, not *were, was* − when he *was* in England. Can you say it correctly now please.

3 IT'S THE SOCIAL MEDIUM

It is how you control pupils and express your relationship with them. If, for example, you say 'Did you have a nice weekend, Rita?' you can very easily be doing two different things. You are either being nice to Rita and taking a personal interest in her or you're practising the past tense!

Remember, you can only exploit the language in the classroom in this way if you are aware of what you're saying and why you're saying it.

4 IT'S YOU

Perhaps the biggest problem is that language is also the principle way most young teachers avoid silence. They hate being in front of a group, with a very loud silence everywhere. So they break it by talking themselves, but unfortunately this raises two problems. Firstly, very few pupils will speak while you are talking so you are actually encouraging their silence. Secondly, they are probably trying to understand what you say − they are treating what you say as either the subject or the medium. Talking to avoid silence makes the situation worse and worse, and means that very often you have to be brave and simply keep quiet.

The worst case which can be very funny to an observer but not to the pupils is the teacher who commentates:

Good morning everybody.
Good morning.
Well, this morning we're going to learn about how to ask people to do things for you. Now let me see, oh dear, the blackboard's in a mess. Where's the duster? Just a minute now, I'll just look for the duster. Um, can anybody see the duster anywhere? Ah, there it is, just a moment, I'll just clean the board and then I'll put the heading up for you . . . There we are, now that's the board cleaned. Now, um . . . where's the chalk . . . here we are. Now . . . 'Asking people to do things for you'.

The teacher has said all that and, for most of the pupils at least, it has meant absolutely nothing − except that the teacher appeared confused and, worse, the pupils are now thoroughly confused too. What is going on?

Equally tempting is to explain (to yourself) what is going to happen next:

Now, I'm going to give you this text and I want you to read it and when you've read it I'm going to ask you some questions and I want you to answer them. So, I'll give you the text now.

What a surprise! You may have reassured yourself but you also confused (and probably amused) the pupils too.

You will find it helpful to bear the following in mind when teaching language.

(a) Be concrete
Start by talking about the pupils' own experiences not abstract questions. Start, as well, with questions the answers to which are linguistically simple (*yes* or *no*, or a single word or short phrase). Do not expect people to answer 'clever' questions at the beginning of what you are saying. Pupils face two problems – thinking out something worth saying AND having the English available to say it.

(b) Don't try to be 'intellectual'
As a direct follow-up to (a) if you try to be deep or 'interesting', at least at the beginning, you will simply be asking too much of people. Don't be afraid to be banal and straightforward when you start.

(c) Listen and respond
The response should be appropriate in two ways – both as a teacher (by, for example, correcting them or following up with a further question) and as a person. It's very easy to make this sort of mistake:

You	Do you go to the cinema very often?
Pupil 1	No, not really.
You	What about you?
Pupil 2	Yes, quite often.
You	How often?
Pupil 2	Oh about once a week.
You	What about you?
Pupil 3	No, not much but I was in a film once.
You	Oh were you? And what about you?
Pupil 4	I prefer to watch television . . . .

It must be obvious that the pupil who volunteered '*I was in a film once*' is not going to volunteer much more if all the teacher says is '*Oh were you*'. Take a normal human interest in what the pupils say.

(d) Correct
This shows that you are listening and are competent. It does not mean you have to jump on every mistake but if pupils know themselves that they have made mistakes and you just nod or say 'Good, good', or 'Oh really, did you', they will very quickly think that you are neither interested nor competent.

(e) Be explicit
There are several different reasons for saying something in the language classroom. It's important for you to separate these clearly for the pupils.

(f) Change your voice
If you listen to one of the good television news readers, not only do they sound relatively spontaneous but it is also easy to hear when they change from one item to another or when, for example, they quote somebody else's words. Because you're using language for several different reasons (often at the same time) you must change your voice too. Make plenty of pauses and change the pitch. Think, for example, how you would say:

No, not buyed, *bought*, I *bought* it in Paris, can you say that please?

Said on a monotone, it's impossible to understand either what you mean or what you want the pupil to do. Use your voice – and in particular use pauses – to make it clear.

6.3 A basic approach

When you start teaching – or even running conversation groups, it's easy to look for 'the' method. But remember, all good teaching or group work is eclectic. It isn't possible to say 'You should *never* do so-and-so'. On the other hand there is a logical pattern which usually applies, from which you should only deviate if you have definite reasons for doing so. It can be summarised as follows:

(a) Find out if the pupils can already do what you have in mind. If they can do it – then you don't do it again. Change your objective to something different (which may of course only be a deeper appreciation of the same thing). If they can't do it carry on with (b).

(b) Present the ideas or material. At this point the teacher dominates the proceedings – often 'talking to himself'. When we're talking about this part of the work below we call it T – T work, Teacher to Teacher.

(c) Ask for some sort of response from the class, or group, without picking on individuals. Now the pupils have come more into the lesson and the teacher is taking a less dominant role. Below we call this part of the approach T – C.

(d) Individual pupils are asked to make some response. Again the emphasis is moving away from the teacher and on to the pupils. We call this phase T – P.

(e) The pupils work together – often in pairs – doing something with the language. The teacher is taking an even less dominant role. We call this part P – P.

(f) The teacher finally 'loses control' completely. The pupils work together in what appears to be an uncontrolled way. The pupils are working together in groups or individually and the teacher himself is frequently not using any language at all at this point. He's going round the room helping individuals or listening to the groups, but now the pupils dominate the activity completely.

Remember, one part at least of learning to use a foreign language involves some sort of mimicry (though, of course, that's by no means the whole story) and this basic approach is little more than a sophisticated version of *say after me*. The teacher presents, the class does something, the individuals do something and, finally, we hope the pupils are actually using language, including some new language which they have just integrated into what they already knew, in a natural, or at least quasi–natural, way.

This pattern is no absolute guide. Like notes, which may help you to better organisation but which may equally 'cramp your style' and lose the spontaneity of what you're doing, so the

pattern we have just mentioned can have the same effect. The best rule is to respond naturally but, if you find it difficult to get a response yourself, ask yourself if you are jumping too many steps in the basic approach.

6.4 Controlling your own language

We have seen already that when you use English in an English as a Foreign Language classroom you are using it for several different purposes at the same time, and it's important to try to separate these. The assistant is, from the beginning, in a rather difficult role – nobody's quite sure whether he is a student or a teacher or whatever. The pupils, however, will tend to see you as a teacher – as somebody who is supposed to be in control.

In this short section of the book we try to show you how to control your own language. Sometimes we present a transcription of how a teacher uses language. We have tried to present these to show stress, pauses, and so on. You will understand the effects best if you can imagine a classroom situation and read the transcripts aloud.

1 LANGUAGE FOR GIVING INSTRUCTIONS

Avoid long-winded polite requests. The simplest method of giving instructions is to use the imperative – but avoid shouting instructions out like orders.

Turn to page 44 . . . 44 . . . look at the examples there . . . at the top of the page . . . Listen!

Remember, the secret with giving instructions is to use the minimum possible number of words. At the risk of stating the obvious, here are some more examples:

Look at me please . . .
Don't look at your books yet . . . just listen.
Work in pairs – you two (pointing), you two . . .
I'll read that again

This time listen carefully for/to . . .
You have two or three minutes to look at that,
then I'll go through it with you.

2 LANGUAGE FOR HIGHLIGHTING

To point out a problem, an example, or an important point, pause *before* and then change pitch on the word or phrase. This makes it easy to separate from the flow of speech and therefore easy to follow.

Look at the top of page 48, there are two examples there. Listen to them . . . He knows her doesn't he . . . He KNOWS her DOESN'T he . . . Here's the second one . . . He doesn't know her does he . . . He DOESN'T know her DOES he . . . Notice the verbs . . . Doesn't . . . Does . . . Does . . . Doesn't . . . If the main sentence is positive, the tag is negative. If the main sentence is negative, the tag is positive. Listen again. He doesn't know her does he . . . doesn't, does.

This is explicit. It is broken into short phrases and the important words clearly stressed and highlighted.

3 THE LANGUAGE OF CORRECTING

Very often when a pupil makes a mistake he already <u>knows</u> what he should have said — it's a slip of the tongue and a long explanation is NOT necessary. The pupil needs the practice not you. So he MUST repeat the correct form and not just the correct form in isolation, but in context. Here is a transcription of a good correction:

T   Where did he buy it?
P   He buyed it from London.
T   *From* London?
P   Yes.
T   No, not *from, in*. Can you say it please, *in* London.
P   *In* London.
T   That's right. Where did he buy it?
P   He buyed it *in* London.

T   Yes, but we don't say *buyed*. We say . . . anybody?
P2 *Bought.*
T   Good. That's right. *Bought*. It's an irregular verb. So where did he buy it?
P   He *buyed* it in London.
T   No, not *buyed, bought*. Say it please.
P   *Bought.*
T   All of it please.
P   He *bought* it in London.
T   Good. So where did he buy it?
P   He *bought* it in London.

Written out this may seem slow, laborious and rather boring, but the way it is done involves everyone and done fairly quickly, it is much more interesting than a long explanation from you.

4 THE LANGUAGE OF EXPLAINING

Explaining need not necessarily be done linguistically. It is comical to watch a teacher explain 'a watch' while wearing one! Remember, too, that you are not usually explaining to the pupils what, for example, a watch *is*. Frequently you are only 'telling them the word', not explaining anything.

You may think that the easiest way to explain is to translate but we have discussed why it's not a good idea for you to reveal to the pupils how much of their language you know (although in a few cases translation is inevitable).

Ways of explaining words
(a) demonstration
eg grin, angry, hop, stagger
(Most verbs, most nouns, and many adjectives can be explained in this way).

(b) drawing
eg slim, tree, bush, yacht
(A quick sketch with a few lines, it only has to show the essential details).

(c) opposites
eg if you are single you're not married; Jack is polite, but his brother is rude

(Notice they do not need to be logical opposites in the strict sense. In the same way as the tree/bush drawings the secret is to contrast two words, one the pupils know and the new word to highlight the difference).

(d) synonyms
eg huge means very big
plump means fat
(Again, they are often not exact synonyms. The idea is to give the pupils the general meaning of the word. This is not an exercise in logic).

(e) definitions
eg an optician is a man who tests your eyes and tells you if you need glasses
(It's usually much more difficult to give definitions than to use (a) to (d)).

(f) give a context
eg Someone who doesn't say sorry when he bumps into you is rude.
Someone is rude when they don't apologise when they're late or if they push past you in a crowd.
(Here you must always give several contexts to make sure the word is not misunderstood).

(g) translation
eg oak, measles, alsatian
(This is mostly used for words which are 'a kind of dog/disease/etc.' Even here if you want to avoid speaking the pupils' language in class you can say to one of the pupils, *Could you look that up in the dictionary for us, please. What's the (German) word for it?*)

(h) explaining grammar
To explain a grammar point or what we say in a given situation can be more difficult than explaining vocabulary. Again, however, there are tactics to reduce the amount of language you use. The most important are:

(i) use questions and answers − ask yourself a question and answer it: 'Why do we use *any* in this sentence, not *some*? It's because the sentence is negative.'
'Why do we use *excuse me*, not *sorry* here? It's because something is GOING to happen. We use *excuse me* BEFORE something, but *sorry* after.'

(ii) With advanced classes you can use the question and answer technique by asking the class the same sort of question. If someone in the class answers, it saves you explaining something they already know and gives them a chance to talk, instead of you (but if you ask the class the general question *What does . . . mean?* you will almost never get an answer, even if they do know. It is very difficult to define words in a foreign language. Your questions should always be of the kind, *Why do we say/use . . ., not . . . here?* Thus the answer they have to give is linguistically simple, even if the idea behind it is quite difficult.

(iii) Draw attention to an example in context: '*Did you notice* what I/he said? (. . . what it said in the text?)'
'*I/he/it said* . . . When we want to . . . we say . . .'
Notice this needs very little language indeed:
'When we want to ask if we can do something, we say *Do you mind if I . . .*'

(iv) When you are presenting grammar present only the part that is relevant to the problem. Make simple statements that are true but perhaps not the whole truth. Try to say something the pupils can use without worrying if it is complete. You should say as little as possible, which should be as concise as possible. If the language of the explanation is more difficult than the point you are explaining something is wrong.

5 THE LANGUAGE FOR DOING EXERCISES

Once more, the pupil needs the practice not you! Here is a short transcript of a well-presented exercise. Notice again, how little the teacher says.

Practice
Look at these two patterns:

DO you mind if I HAVE a chocolate?
WOULD you mind if I HAD a chocolate?
Use those two patterns when you want to:
1 Phone someone later.
2 Use the telephone.
3 Leave early.
4 Put the light on.
5 Take it home with you.
6 Ring a friend.
7 Smoke.
8 Have some more.

T   So, notice if it starts with DO it's followed by the present . . . DO you mind if I HAVE . . . but if it starts with WOULD it's followed by the PAST . . . WOULD you mind if I HAD . . . Now look at exercise *7(c)*. Can you do the first one please, Maurice? Start *do*.

P1 Do you mind if I phone you later?

T   Good. The same one, Danielle. Start with *would*, please.

P2 Would you mind if I phone you later?

T   It's the past if you start with *would*. Do it again please.

P2 Would you mind if I phoned you later?

T   Good. Number 2, Robert. Start *do* . . .

Exercise 4

Start your answer with 'I'll probably . . .'
What will you do:
1 If it rains tomorrow.
2 When you get home this evening.
3 At the weekend.
4 If you feel ill in the morning.
5 Next summer.
6 If you win a lot of money.

T   So if we want to talk about something we're not sure about, something that MIGHT happen, we can use — *I'll*

probably. Let's look at exercise 4. Can you do number 1, please, Maria.

P1 *(silence)*.

T   If it rains tomorrow what will you do. Start *I'll probably*.

P1 I'll probably, er, I'll probably bring my umbrella.

T   Good. Can you say something different, Mario?

P2 I'll probably stay at home.

T   Oh you will, will you, have a day off school, um hum. Can you do number 2 then please. Yes, you again, Mario.

P2 I'll probably go to sleep, I'm tired.

T   Very good Mario. The same one, Antonio.

P3 I'll probably have something to eat.

T   Good — the same one then, Arthur.

P4 I'll probably go to see my grandmother.

T   Good. Number 3, Silvio . . .

With exercises which require a personal response, each example can be used several times. Obviously, exercises like this have more opportunity for some humour and, if the opportunity for a little 'conversation' comes up, interrupt the exercise for a couple of minutes chat and then return to it.

We hope by now we have made clear that we are not suggesting that you control your language as some kind of theoretical principle. On the contrary it's of direct practical help to you in the classroom. The occasional word, gestures and particularly eye movement are often much better than a lot of talk from the teacher.

If you find yourself talking too much, look back at the tactics we have suggested above. Perhaps the most important principle of all is not to be afraid to be quiet. If you are silent the pupils will usually find something to say.

Chapter 7

Preparation and resources

7.1 Resource material

Before you get to Barcelona or Dusseldorf the classes you are going to take probably seem rather remote, but remember that while you are in Britain and before you go you are surrounded by English language materials and a host of ordinary things which will make your lessons easier for you and more interesting and concrete for the pupils. So it is worth giving some thought, while you still have the chance to do something about it, to the sort of things you may either need, or at least find useful, while you are out there.

OFFICIAL PAPERS

Apart from the personal things you take, it will probably be a good idea to take a number of copies of the sort of free official information which you can easily get from information offices, railway stations, post offices, travel agents, theatres and so on. If you do take such things you need enough of them (if they're going to have one each) or be large enough (if you're going to have a group looking at them). Remember, too, that you will need spare copies for those that get damaged or lost.

We suggest the following may be useful:

1   Pocket timetables from your local railway station – perhaps to and from London, or another big city.
2   Copies of the railway brochure about what kind of ticket you need.
3   Brochures about obtaining inter-rail passes (if you're going to have pupils who are old enough to do so themselves).
4   Pocket maps of the London underground (available from the information bureaus on most of the bigger underground stations). Alternatively, a large map of the underground system. The best, because they are so durable, are those printed on tea towels. These can usually be bought in big stores for about a pound.
5   Maps of London. You can usually obtain these free from the London Tourist Board.
6   Brochures advertising guided tours – either of London, or a town near where you live, or even an area of the country near where you live. If you live in a 'tourist town' it's usually possible to get a *What's On* brochure or card which is displayed in local shops. You will find that materials you have found which the pupils will see as the real thing are better than anything which you can take from any book.
7   From any tourist town near where you live, several maps of the town and/or brochures about local services.
8   A store guide from any large department store you visit (the little brochure which shows what floor the different departments are on etc.).
9   Information about the opening times and facilities of any local attraction near where you live – a country house, a zoo, a museum, or whatever. It is not particularly important when choosing these that the place is one that your pupils might want to visit. You use them as a concrete basis for situations (see chapter 3).
10   The poster or guide for foreign students on how to use an English telephone – you could ask at your local post office for one of these. Alternatively, there is a brochure called *Using the telephone – a leaflet for students*. This and similar materials for use in schools are available if you write to your

Telephone Manager or Head Postmaster.

11 In addition to the *What's On* guide we suggested above, several (different) copies of the entertainment guide from your local paper can be a good idea. It may be worth mentioning that the local paper is usually better than the national paper here as it usually has a wider range in a smaller area of paper than, for example, the London Theatre Guide in the national press. Remember, too, that the latter will probably be rather outside the experience of most of your pupils and the page from the local paper with cinemas, discos, clubs, and so on will probably be more practical. In the same way it can be a good idea to take several pages from the paper listing the evening's or weekend's television programmes.

12 One of the main problems people face when they go abroad is feeding themselves, and their most immediate problem is often understanding a menu − particularly a 'pub lunch' or snack bar menu. The whole thing will be much more realistic if you are prepared to write out the menu yourself on cards. Most pubs have these supplied to them and a request at your local will probably get you half a dozen blank cards.

INFORMATION ABOUT YOUR HOST COUNTRY

Pupils are very often interested in information − particularly if it's inaccurate! − about their own country. While you are in England you will obviously find it easier to get English language material about, for example, France. There are four obvious sources:

(a) The French Consulate − write and ask for any information they have in English about the part of France you are going to.

(b) Your local travel agent. Here you should find a number of brochures advertising trips to different parts of your host country. Most of them will have little descriptions of the area with the main tourist attractions mentioned.

(c) Most books used in schools now for teaching French have some information about France. If you have a younger brother or sister who is using a textbook take copies of the pages that give information about 'Marcel's typical day at school' or other pieces of information which purport to represent typical French life. Notice you can use these even if they are in French − the pupils can then tell you whether the French is correct or not and whether the information contained in the book is correct or not. In most cases that should stimulate comment!

(d) You should be keeping your eye on the English newspapers for articles and news items about your host country. Remember, you are not usually looking for long, thoughtful, analytical articles. Much more useful are short news items. The ideal is the short news item which displays a clear 'prejudice' about the host country. Needless to say, you should avoid ones that are particularly topical and will therefore seem dated if used in six months' time. If anything of particular interest happens in the country you're going to visit in the months before you go there it's worth buying several newspapers − a variety of quality papers and the more popular press − and taking out different articles about the same incident, topic or personality.

BOOKS

It would be easy to give a long list of books which may be of use. We have tried to avoid that. The policy we have employed here is to exclude as many books as possible. Most of you will find that the school has an extensive library of basic textbooks, dictionaries and grammar books. To be realistic, you will not want to spend a lot of money taking books which *may* be useful. Please read the notes we have added to the various books here. Think in advance of the age and level of your pupils and try to take only those things that you really will use. At the same time, most of the books recommended here will be difficult to get in the majority of European towns. We cannot emphasise too strongly that an investment of about £10 before you go will save you many hours of worry preparing classes.

General introduction
Apart from the information you will have received from the Central Bureau, there is only one book published in England specifically for the assistant – *A Handbook for English Language Assistants* by R. R. Jordan and R. McKay (Collins).

This contains a certain amount of practical information about, for example, the French and German school systems. It also offers concrete advice particularly suited to those teaching younger pupils. In part, it covers similar ground to this book though not always from the same point of view.

Books strongly recommended for all assistants
Make Your Point by L. G. Alexander and M. C. Vincent (Longman).

This gives thirty discussion topics for students at secondary level. It has a clear introduction suggesting how the particular topics may be used. Suitable for intermediate students.

How to Say it by Philip Binham (Longman).
A really excellent little book with pronunciation, stress and conversation practices, suitable for all levels of class. Has good notes to guide you and tells you what to do and how to do it.

English Conversation Practice by K. Methold (Longman).
This book presents a series of short dialogues in excellent natural English suitable for teaching most classes. There are extensive notes on language points and good practices. Although you may not be able to use some of the material directly, it should prove an excellent source book and help you with some of the intricacies of normal spoken English.

Oral Drills in Sentence Patterns by Helen Monfries (Macmillan).
This book contains a large number of oral grammar practices. In each case there is a short and extremely clear introduction for you. The examples are systematically arranged and easy to use. If there is one book you take with you, this should be it.

English Teaching Games and Contests by W. R. Lee (OUP).
There are a number of 'games' books. This is probably the best known and most useful.

What Do You think? by D. Byrne and A. Wright (Longman).
These are a series of three books (called Books 1, 2 and 3) of pictures. There is no text in the book at all. The pictures are of different kinds – drawings, photographs, diagrams, etc. and can be used for different kinds of work. At least one of the books should prove invaluable.

A more unusual book which you may find more difficult to get (you are more likely to find it in the puzzle section of W. H. Smith than in a specialist bookshop) is:

Solve-a-Crime by A. C. Gordon (W. Foulsham and Co. Ltd., Yeoville Road, Slough, Bucks.).
This book is discussed and one of the stories reproduced on p. 96. You should find it useful for listening comprehension and stimulating the interest generally of all except the youngest pupils (it also has the advantage of being very cheap)!

Course books
There is clearly no necessity for you to take a course book to use in class. At the same time, you may find that the text books are very old-fashioned and that you want to present items which seem a bit more useful and relevant but are rather short of ideas on what to present and in what order. In those circumstances you will probably find it useful to have a textbook for

your own reference. We recommend you take *not more than two* of the following – choosing them according to the age and level of your posting.

Kernel 1 by Robert O'Neill (Longman).

A new and extremely well-thought-out course for beginners in which every sentence of the book is useful from the very first. Superb source of good practices which you could use with less able or younger pupils.

English in Situations by Robert O'Neill (OUP).

A rather off-putting looking book, very serious, but full of excellent practices at intermediate and upper intermediate levels. Very useful for those going to secondary schools (and, because of its systematic approach, particularly for those going to Germany).

A Holiday English Language Programme by Mark Fletcher and John Buss (Hodder and Stoughton).

This book is basically intended for students on summer courses, but has a lot of bits in it that may give you useful activities to do in class. The level is lower intermediate and the style probably well suited to your needs.

Another similar book is:

Activities by Bernard Seal (Longman).

Two more for which you may have use are as follows:

For and Against by L. G. Alexander (Longman).

This consists of thirty discussion topics presented extensively for advanced students only. The topics are difficult and only suitable for pupils at the highest level. On the other hand, if you expect to have such classes it will produce more demanding discussion lessons than we have suggested here.

Modern English Pronunciation Practice by Munro Mackenzie (Longman).

An extremely small (pocket-sized) book full of pronunciation practice. If you expect to have younger children and want more material than we suggest this book provides

enough for a whole year in an easily accessible and usable form.

For those going into language teaching

Many people studying modern languages and working abroad as assistants intend to become language teachers – either of their target language, or of English as a Foreign Language. If you are interested from this point of view you will find the following worthwhile reading while you are abroad, but we stress that in no sense are these intended to help you directly with your work as an assistant (they are also inevitably somewhat more expensive than the books we have recommended above).

Linguistics in Language Teaching by D. A. Wilkins (Edward Arnold) and indeed almost anything else written by D. A. Wilkins.

English as a Foreign Language by R. A. Close (Allen & Unwin 3rd ed.).

The best, most practical and above all most accurate introduction to English grammar and how it should be approached by the EFL teacher.

The most comprehensive introduction to language teaching is an American publication widely available in Britain:

Teaching Foreign Language Skills by Wilga Rivers (Chicago University Press).

Magazines

The following will prove a source of useful ideas:

Modern English Teacher, available from Modern English Publications Ltd, 33 Shaftesbury Avenue, London W1V 7DD.

Catch, Current, Crown, Clockwork, Club, etc. – a series of magazines usually appearing nine times a year and available from Mary Glasgow Publications Ltd, 140 Kensington Church Street, London W8 4BM.

Miscellaneous materials you can collect

The items that follow do not fit into any particular pattern but are all things which are easy to obtain in Britain and which make it much easier to teach one or more lessons from the concrete plans we offered in chapter 3.

(a) A plastic outline stencil of your host country (these are normally available very cheaply from, for example, W. H. Smith).

(b) Two or three English greeting cards – the card that differs most from European cards is a Valentine card.

(c) Several pictures that are 'typically English' – if you keep your eye on the colour supplements and other magazines which you see around your home you will find pictures which are unmistakably English. A small group of such pictures is very useful (see p. 38).

(d) Any questionnaires that appear in magazines (even if some of the questions are not suitable for use in class).

(e) One or two books of language puzzles (but not crosswords). Particularly if you're going to teach younger children you will find that these books provide a source of materials and, perhaps above all, a source of ideas for the kind of language games you can make up yourself. The most likely place to find such books is in the children's department of any good bookshop.

(f) A small number of teenage magazines aimed at the age group you're going to teach, or at an age group that is slightly younger than the one you are going to teach – remember, there will be a language problem as well.

(g) Any 'cornflake packet problem' you see between now and going (see p. 52).

(h) Any short letters to the press which express strong views about topics you think will be within the capabilities of the age group you're going to teach (again, if it's a real letter out of the newspaper it provides a more concrete basis for discussion than something you merely make up).

(i) Pictures of well-known people.

7.2 Making a tape

Many of you probably have a cassette tape recorder and are thinking of taking it with you for your year abroad. If so, a few short tapes prepared in advance while you're still in England will provide variety and extra interest for your lessons. Here are a few ideas for things you could record:

1 Four or five different native speakers from different parts of the country who have distinguishable accents yet still speak clearly. You could also add one person (perhaps your grandmother or an uncle) who has a much stronger accent.

2 One or two older people talking about how things have changed.

3 With two or three friends record some short (six to ten line) dialogues which illustrate the language mentioned in chapter 3. You will find these dialogues most natural if you record them using an outline script, but allow the people who are speaking on the tape to deviate slightly from the script if they find it more natural to add a word, take a word away, pause or whatever. Needless to say, you should then make sure before you use them in class that you are certain of the *exact* words that are used on the tape.

4 Perhaps the most effective of all recorded materials is if you interview people who have lived in your host country. You should ask them to express one or two views which are decisive enough to prompt correction or opposition from the class. The ideal people to interview for this purpose are probably students back at the university who have spent a year as an assistant and therefore have some idea of how difficult the language they use can be, so that the interviews are difficult enough to keep pupils interested but easy enough not to be outside their range.

5 If you are going to teach older, more capable students, a short recording of three or four people discussing their attitudes to the host country (or any other question for that matter) can be helpful. It is, however, very difficult for students to follow a discussion with three or four native speakers speaking naturally together, so you should only use this for pupils in the last years of school when you are sure that it will not be beyond them.

Any tape you make should be short, or at least easily divisible into short (2–5 minute) sections. Listening to a tape of a native speaker can be very difficult indeed for the pupils and you must never use more than a few minutes of tape in any lesson.

Remember, a couple of hours before you leave university spent with some friends who are also going abroad preparing a tape will probably save you a lot of evenings trying to dream up something to do once you get out to your host country. A couple of half-hour cassettes of varied spoken materials should provide the basis for a dozen or more lessons.

There are three things you can do while still in this country which will ensure that you enjoy your time abroad more and are more effective, both in your classes and in your own learning of your target language:

(a) Go and *listen* – to ordinary people using English, particularly acquaintances and strangers. Try to get some feel for what does sound natural and what does not. Do not concern yourself with studying the grammar, but rather try to make sure that you can guide your pupils accurately towards the sort of language that they should use in everyday situations.

(b) Go and *collect* the various materials we've listed below, bearing in mind of course that only a selection of them will be suitable for the particular age level that you are going to meet.

(c) Go and *think* about what you're going to do in some of your first classes. Do not wait until you get out to the foreign country and then start to worry. Plan a few lessons while you're still in England – of course you may change your mind completely once you get abroad, but at least you will have thought some things out and, if you need any special materials you will have taken them with you. As usual, the more concrete your preparation, the more effective it's likely to be and the more relaxed and effective you are likely to be.